Brushing Fire

Soul Poetry
by
Anna Marie Kittrell

First Edition, 2015

Published in the United States of America

Author contact info: kittrellbooks@gmail.com

Facebook.com/AKittrell

DEDICATION

For my great-grandmother, Dessie Inez Deatherage.
January 07, 1913—July 20, 1994

Thank you, Grandma, for introducing me to the One who paints with fire.

FOR THE READER

This collection is a glimpse into my soul. Portions whispered to the page in a still, small voice. Others shouted like a trumpet blast. All were written under the influence of the Holy Spirit.

May God bless your heart and speak to your soul as you read Brushing Fire, just as He did to mine as I wrote it.

Visionary

Wind-whipped pigtails in the grass
I stretch out on the lawn
Hot summer days and my front teeth
Too quickly will be gone

Will You step out upon this cloud
As I watch from below?
I bug my eyes and crane my neck
As far as it will go

Sunspots swim before my eyes
Freckles dot my cheeks
Fluffy animals drift by
With wings and tails and beaks

My brown eyes dart and circle round
The sky of snow cone blue
I know if I look hard enough
I'll catch a glimpse of You

Many suns have ventured through
So many August skies
My thoughts have found You many times
But never have my eyes

Lawn lounging lost appeal to me
Pigtails escaped my hair
But how I love blue summer skies
And still search for You there

I know one day while gazing up
A God-shaped cloud I'll see
I'll dance and twirl like a little girl
When You come back for me

Persistent Peace

My voice is clear
A beautiful melody
Rich with emotion

I call to your heart

You listen with your ears
Unable to hear My song
The song created

Especially for you

Take a quiet moment
Pull it from your day
Make it your own

Then give it to Me

In Worship
And in Praise
And I will give you Peace

Unlike the world gives

Persistent Peace
With mercy new
Every morning

Listen with your heart

In Search of the One

Shepherd, where are You? Your work is not done
I'm out in the wilderness, searching for one
Who minds Your flock till the late setting sun?
They tend one another as I search for one
You search for one lost, but the ninety-nine shun?
Ninety-nine know I'd seek them, if they were the one
But how can You trust the free flock not to run?
They remember not long ago, they were the one
What if they turn from this life You've begun?
Then I'll search for one hundred lost sheep, one by one

My flock knows the sound of the voice of God's Son
As the Shepherd of Souls, My work is not done
With love strong and grace gentle the battles are won
The earth and its powers will soon be undone
Until then you will find Me, in search of the one

A Gift Made For Giving

I remember the day
When you whispered My name
Your shoulders weighed down
With your burden of shame

Your head hung down low
As your eyes brimmed with tears
At My feet you let go
Of pain harbored for years

Your heart was so cluttered
With sorrow and sin
Still, as I stood knocking
You beckoned Me in

Your burden soon lifted
You walked upon air
The gift of forgiveness
I offered you there

I remember your eyes
Flaming bright like the sun
Your praise-laden tongue
Longed to tell everyone

A chorus of angels
Sang out with one voice
When a lost child comes home
All the heavens rejoice

Share the gift you received
On your day of rebirth
Humbly offer forgiveness
To all on this earth

Daughter

I shall paint a new sunrise
For a brand new pair of eyes
A little one is born into My earth

Her morning sky I'll color blue
Her eyes will match the sapphire hue
My birds will sing in tribute to her birth

I'll ask My flowers to spring up
Her favorite is the buttercup
Their sunny smiles will brighten up her day

And in the night when she can't sleep
Because in darkness shadows creep
I'll close her eyes and dream her fears away

As she learns and as she grows
Strength and godliness she shows
With tenderness, I'll hold her gentle hand

When youthful days leave her behind
I will turn her troubled mind
To thoughts of life within My Beulah Land

I will paint a new sunrise
For a brand new pair of eyes
The child I dearly love is on her way

I'll open up the gates of pearl
To welcome home My little girl
My daughter comes to live with Me today

Childish

God, don't let me skin my knee
If I fall down during P.E.

Please help me to do my best
On my Social Studies test

I pray the homeless man in town
Will find a job and settle down

Will take a wife and have a son
Get time to laugh and have some fun

I pray that everyone I know
Will follow Christ and learn to grow

That none will turn away and leave
The world will listen and believe

When Mom and Daddy roll their eyes
And think I'm too young to be wise

Or think my prayers are out of reach
Let my example lead and teach

I am weak but He is strong
Having faith is never wrong

Heaven holds the meek and mild
Who enter as a little child

Freckle Faith

I am just a little girl
With freckles on my nose
I'd walk a mile in pouring rain
To pick my mom a rose

Although I'm in the second grade
My soul is very wise
You will find no prejudice
Or judgment in my eyes

I'll grow up to be an artist
And a dancer and a vet
I have more than fifty friends
Though I haven't met them yet

I'm uncomfortable in public
Sometimes I growl and glare
I pretend that I'm an animal
Being shy is hard to bear

But please be gentle with me
My heart is small, you know
And Jesus loves me very much
My Bible tells me so

And though my smile is missing teeth
My spirit's filled with glee
For all who enter Heaven
Must become a child, like me

A Mother's Heart

A movement within

I close my eyes and imagine Your tiny face

I trace unseen hands and feet across my skin

My finger longs to feel the curl of Your warm little fist

A gentle flutter brings a smile

What are You doing in there? I wonder

A tiny little heart so full of love, beating out a message that will

Save the world

Can You hear my voice?

I sing a lull-a-bye to the small, sweet ears of a listening babe

I feel the gentle pressure as You stretch out Your tiny arms

One day You will stretch them out for me as the sin of the world

Rests upon Your innocent shoulders

I long for the day I will hold You peacefully in my arms

And can look into Your trusting eyes

But for now I will hold You within

Safe and sound

And let Your warmth comfort me

Stillness

The stillness of town Bethlehem
Its doors all bolted tight
No room to host a baby's birth
As Joseph knocked that night

The stillness of a shining star
Above a newborn king
In silent awe the shepherds stopped
To hear the angels sing

The stillness of young Mary's heart
She pondered on God's plan
While quieting the hungry cries
Of Jesus, Son of Man

The stillness of the breath of God
As Christ was crucified
Guiltless blood shed for our souls
Poured forth from His pierced side

The stillness of the angel
As he sat upon the stone
Christ's gift to us, an empty grave
Through death His love was shown

Special Deliverer

I'm certain Mary paused to count
Ten wrinkled, wiggling toes
Before she snugly tucked You in
Your infant swaddling clothes

Surely, she caressed Your cheek
And kissed Your tender brow
As wise men traveled through the night
To greet You with a bow

She pondered in her humble heart
God's miracle foretold
As earthly father, Joseph, stood
In honor, manifold

She must have hugged You to her chest
As night fell, dark and deep
Her lullaby soothed Godly tears
As she sang You to sleep

Around her mortal fingertip
A Savior's fist was curled
For Mary held within her hands
The hands that hold the world

The Understanding

Take Your hands from my flaw
Please don't touch me there
Turn Your face—avert Your eyes
Your scrutiny I can't bear

Hold Your tongue—hold Your peace
Please don't say a word
Keep Your judgments to yourself
Swallow them, unheard

Calloused hands scarred in love
Would dare not touch my skin
Scars deform my very soul
Not scars of love, but sin

He cupped my chin, searched my eyes
Held me to His chest
Each flaw within my blistered heart
He tenderly caressed

I shook my head—I creased my brow
My tears began to flow
No words of judgment stung my ear
He simply said, "I know."

Lost

To be lost in You, Lord
Like a treasured book's page
One I cannot put down
Growing fonder with age

Lost in a valley
Hidden from view
Living on manna
Provided by You

Let me be lost
From myself without care
Apart from this costume
Of flesh that I wear

Lost like a raindrop
Blown free by the wind
A drink for dry land
To go where You send

Help me get lost
From this world that I'm in
To be pleaser of God
Not a pleaser of men

Lost in a crowd
With my mind upon You
To lose myself, Lord
Is the least I can do

Blessing River

Your blessings are a river
Alive and flowing free
A wide and constant stream of hope
Submerging all of me

Bathed in Your Living Water
I breathe grace out and in
My will is drowned within Your depths
My soul, washed free from sin

At times I cling to trouble
As it comes bobbing by
Concerns float all around me
With doubts that terrify

Weighed down with needless worry
I soon begin to sink
Forgetting I'm adrift within
The well from which I drink

Freedom comes from letting go
I smile and dive right down
Into the Blessing River deep
The sweetest place to drown

Reminder

Thank You, my Lord, for appearing
And taking me out of my mind
For showing Your work all around me
Revealing Your perfect design

I welcome Your pleasant distraction
This much needed moment of praise
A reminder of how big Your love is
And how short the grief of my days

With care You design every creature
Each face is carved by Your own hand
You never forget one expression
Found on the face of beast or man

A great big world filled with small beings
Spinning with pleasure and pain
You propelled our world into orbit
And on us Your hand will remain

I see You atop every mountain
I picture You in every cloud
I find You within Your creation
Your still, small voice shouting out loud

Thank You, my Lord, for Your constant
And unchanging mercy and grace
You grant me much needed forgiveness
My sins You completely erase

A Servant's Prayer

You walked across the hot, dry sand
To free the tired and weak
And it would be my pleasure, Lord
If I could wash Your feet

You strolled upon the angry waves
Not turning in retreat
And it would be my privilege, Lord
If I could wash Your feet

You bore Your cross to Calvary
My needs You died to meet
And I would be most humbled, Lord
If I could wash Your feet

You stood before an empty grave
To claim my soul complete
And it would be an honor, Lord
If I could wash Your feet

Heaven's floors are golden
With no dust upon the street
Your perfect, holy being
Need not bathe in ointment, sweet

But here within my grateful heart
I bow and wash Your feet

Light of Darkness

In the shadows dark, beneath the trees

Sunlight cannot fall

Shadowy places dim with mystery

Roots grow, twisted and gnarled

Underneath the darkened earth

Holding the majestic trees upright

The heads of the trees are held up to the sun

The feet of the trees are buried below

The Creator who blessed the head

Is the Creator who buried the feet

He who dwells in the light

Illuminates the dark places also

Lord of all—I worship You

Go With the Flow

My heart beats with thanks
Knowing from whom blessings flow
I look up

Your blessings flow down
Caught on my tongue like snowflakes
They fill me

You bless so much more
Than just my food and my drink
All is blessed

I stand unworthy
Still You bless my every breath
With Your love

Renewing my strength
Blessing this vapor of life
All my days

The glory is Yours
All shall bow to You my King
Yet, You bless

Summer Wind

Breathing in the morning breeze
As it whispers through the trees
Fresh air heals as I draw in
My clouded head is clear again

In my heart God's blessings dwell
Released in praise as I exhale
Precious is each praise-filled breath
Halted only by my death

By faith I breathe You in and out
That I don't pollute with doubt
The cleansing winds that blow between
The eyes of man and things unseen

In my soul, I seek Your breeze
The gust that brings me to my knees
As I rise and dance within
Your sweetly scented summer wind

Day Maker

The promise of a new day
Is no promise at all
I do not know the hour of life
When God will choose to call

Give me this day, my daily bread
Help me share it with my neighbor
Let my attitude reflect Your love
As I rest, and wake, and labor

Let me do well the job at hand
And whistle while I work
Please help me to find peace of mind
Where dark doubt-shadows lurk

Let me express deep gratitude
When things are going well
And bless my eyes with wisdom
To see under sorrow's veil

For behind the tears of heartache
Rests a rainbow in the soul
We must seek the Lord's own purpose
In the trials we can't control

I will not fear the day at hand
My gift from God above
My days are surely numbered
By the faithful One I love

So Lord, help me remember
When starting out my day
To hold onto Your helping hand
And let You lead the way

Peace

Peace in the valley
Peace in my soul
Peace in this world
Spinning out of control

Peace in the family
Peace between men
Peace breathing out
Peace breathing in

Peace as I'm living
Peace as I die
Peace, fill my heart
And each tear that I cry

Peace, pull me closer
Peace, ease my fear
Peace, make my pathways
And skies remain clear

Peace unlike man gives
Peace from the King
Peace of my Savior
To whom I will cling

Peace, close my eyelids
Peace, bring me rest
Peace of mind, Jesus
My humble request

I Wonder

Jesus, You are close to me
Your Spirit's in my heart
But if You lived on earth today
Like You did at the start...

Would we walk arm in arm along
The way friends sometimes do?
Would You look in my eyes and say
"I know, I've been there too," ?

Would You agree with choices made
Those times I didn't pray?
When I ignored divine advice
And flesh got in the way?

Would You hold my face gently
Within Your dear scarred hands?
While my cares slipped forever
From life's harsh worldly demands?

Would Your eyes hold a twinkle?
Could my humor make You smile?
Would You sit down beside me
Just to visit for a while?

Would You write a song for me
And place it in my heart?
If You lived here on earth, my Lord
As You did at the start?

My Father, My Friend

A friend who sticks much closer than a brother
You understand my motives like no other

You place each smile upon my hardened face
You offer me a godly hiding place

Refreshment to my soul in times of drought
Your Word brings solid ground in times of doubt

I chase the air, but yet You cling to me
Your spirit draws me back where I should be

I feel conviction's shadow head to toe
When I'm outside Your will, You let me know

You allow me then to learn from my mistakes
Arresting foolish pride as it awakes

Life is found within Your hand, divine
The very hand that reaches out for mine

I Turn to You

When thoughts turn wicked in my mind

I turn to You

When worldly views turn my eyes blind

I turn to You

When good intentions turn to greed

I turn to You

When loved ones turn to watch me bleed

I turn to You

When friends turn into enemies

I turn to You

When days turn dark and steal my peace

I turn to You

When nothing turns out like I've planned

I turn to You

When I turn loose and take Your hand

I turn to You

More Than Words

Hope is just a page away
Within Your Living Word
My eyes absorb Your counsel
In each line, Your voice is heard

The breath of life to every soul
I hold in earthly hand
I learn of prophets and of kings
And of Salvation's plan

Written by the hand of God
My source of daily bread
Illustrated by God's Son
When for my sins, He bled

Let every word leap from the page
Into my heart of clay
That I may hide each one within
And find You, day by day

Anchor

Sometimes I am a mighty ship upon the raging sea
At times I'm sure a shaky raft is all I'll ever be

To be a humble lifeboat in the ocean would be grand
A self-sacrificing vessel helping other souls to land

Today I wonder how I'll cross waves restless and untamed
No matter how I choose to sail, my anchor stays the same

My anchor is not made of stone, or iron, or heavy steel
It's forged from God's own mind, and through His Word He made it real

In my vain imagination when I'm tempted into sin
God's Word speaks within my conscience and I'm anchored once again

When I drift and Satan whispers, "You cannot reach God anymore"
I wake to find my drifting vessel anchored firmly to the shore

God, forever be my anchor; help me seek Your face each day
Make me strong within my weakness; form the words I cannot say

On the sea without Your anchor I would sink and surely die
So I hold tight to Your anchor, until I meet You in the sky

Renewal

Your breeze is a cool comfort in the morning

A soft caress of air to my soul

A renewing of my spirit

A reminder of Your love

A softly spoken word of encouragement

A lingering melody

I take it with me

A precious gift

From my Father

Earthen Beauty

Carving a place into Your earth
Calling it our own
We boast self-reliance
Yet search for You upon earthly faces
Comparing their eyes to Your sea, Your stars, Your sky
Desiring for Your earth to kiss us back
To hold us gently
Until we fall heavily
Into Your arms

Holy Knees

We fall at Your feet
Tumbling down in worship, or exhaustion
Only You know for sure

It is not how we fall, but how we arise that matters

Taking what belongs to us
Leaving behind what does not
Opening hearts and closing doors

Waking sin where it sleeps
Crushing it with its eyes wide open

Dusting off our knees
Praying they will not be soon soiled

Knowing they will

The Need to Dust
(Gen 3:19)

Lord, You created Adam from the dust upon the ground
And then created Eve, so in Your love they could abound

I would not exist without You, though sometimes that's hard to see
So I'm asking You, Dear Father, to make humble dust of me

Dust is never filled with anger, found with arrogance or pride
Dust will not harbor resentment or hostility inside

To dust we all will be returning, God's Holy Word does say
So remind me, Precious Savior, that I need to dust today

If I could be dust of the earth, so meek, and lying low
I would not worry with what others think…or do…or know

I would not feel self-absorption, but humility instead
As I lie down in contentment, while my brothers on me tread

It is hard to be self-righteous when you're just a piece of dust
We were all so soiled and dirty when our Jesus died for us

With a drink of Living Water, God has turned me into clay
And with mercy new each morning, gives me strength to dust each day

Flood

My soul shines bright within me
Washed clean and polished new
There seems so much to gain today
Now that the rain is through

A heart, once black, beats in me
Now white and pulsing true
No more do I recall the pain
Now that the rain is through

I thought the flood would drown me
As the water level grew
Such breathless fears I can't explain
Now that the rain is through

You must have lingered near me, Lord
And held me close to You
I rest within Your promised peace
Praise God, the rain is through

Empty

Mary squinted at the morning sky
Surprised the sun could even rise at all
In this world where He was crucified
From eyes swollen with grief, more tears did fall

The man who gave her life, no longer lived
She feared to see His body without breath
One final gift to Jesus she would give
Sweet scent of spice to mask the stench of death

A Mother wept for her son, crucified
Her tears mixed with the road dust on her face
"Oh, God, my son was yours, but yet He died
He has grown cold within in this wicked place."

She wishes she had somehow made a stand
And climbed right up the blood soaked, splintered wood
To take His bleeding face into her hands
And whisper words of comfort while she could

Silently the women walked along
Their feet heavy with sorrow and great pain
What in the heavens could have gone so wrong?
For love to die and nothingness remain

The earth quaked suddenly beneath their feet
They trembled and fell breathless to the ground
Quickly now their hearts began to beat
A rumbling as of thunder did resound

A guarded glance toward their loved one's tomb
Revealed the heavy stone was rolled away
Their souls at once were filled with dread and doom
"Thieves have carried off our Lord today."

"His tomb is empty; do not be afraid,"
An angel spoke with raiment white as snow
"He is alive, and mankind's debt is paid
Of His rising all the world will know."

Astonished, overwhelmed, and filled with glee
The women clung to what the angel said
"Praise God, Christ's resurrection all will see!
Lord Jesus now has risen from the dead!"

They turned and ran on legs as light as air
They worshiped God, joy bursting from within
God's miracle they couldn't wait to share
Jesus Christ has freed the world from sin

Rough Wood

A carpenter selects a tree, potential lies within
His mind's eye sees the ending long before his hands begin

First, he must cut down the tree and change its shape and size
So it will serve a purpose, and appeal to others' eyes

Slowly he peels away the bark, so rough, so hard and dry
Weathered by conditions and the years that have passed by

But deep within the calloused skin a softness can be found
An unlearned hand could never free the beauty that is bound

The skilled hands of the Master can smooth the roughest wood
And cause unyielding, hardened hearts to long for peace and good

The carpenter will look upon a gnarled and fruitless tree
And see not what the tree has done, but what the tree could be

The roughest wood will soon emerge most beautiful of all
Because the carpenter could see the rise beyond the fall

The Goodness of The Lord

Before my lungs had air to breathe
Before my eyes could see
The Lord did faithfully bestow
His goodness unto me

Mother had not called my name
My lips had yet to speak
The goodness of the Lord was strong
Although my limbs were weak

As a child, I grew to love
The goodness of the Lord
His will became my heart's desire
His Word my shield and sword

When adulthood came to me
My Master had a plan
I was called to teach God's Truth
Unto my fellow man

Honored to tell others
Of God's mercy and His grace
I thank Him for each rising sun
Each song, each smiling face

Older now, I rest assured
With Christ I'll someday be
Then I will thank Him face to face
For all He's done for me

Of all the treasures in my life
I've cherished and adored
No earthly love can duplicate
The goodness of the Lord

Unchanged

I have no need to "find myself"
I know just where I stand
Why should I seek men's counsel
When Christ Jesus holds my hand?

No need to leave my happy home
To see the world abroad
I see the love surrounding me
Provided by my God

No mystical discoveries
Or soul searching for me
My soul's right where I left it
In the hands that set me free

Scoffers scoff and mockers mock
And doubters burn with rage
But as they boast their disbelief
God's power remains unchanged

By Way of Red

God's provision is a blessing
With His hand, my home is fed
He turns my shadow of transgression
From black to white—by way of red

He is the Lord of my Salvation
The true believers' common thread
With saving grace He cleansed my sins
From black to white—by way of red

I used to follow worldly counsel
Now I follow Christ instead
He changed the color of my soul
From black to white—by way of red

He will not leave me or forsake me
For my life, His blood was shed
I lift in praise two grateful hands
Washed black to white—by way of red

One day I'll go to meet Him
He'll place a crown upon my head
And I'll thank Him with a heart
Turned black to white—by way of red

The Calling

The talents of life
Uniquely assigned to man
Created by God

Facing the challenge
Man rolls up his sleeves and smiles
Relishing the work

Distraction grows dim
Heartbeat erases time's tick
Labor becomes dance

Beautiful is man
Wisely investing his time
In his gift from God

I See Crosses

I see crosses all around
In street sign shadows on the ground

Crosses line the morning sky
On telephone poles soaring high

Crosses jump at me from signs
Within Railroad Crossing lines

Billboard crosses call to me
Emerging from each letter *t*

Crosses brightly shine at night
When headlight beams reflect just right

His love for me is brought to mind
With every single cross I find

Thundersong

Soft sprinkling shower
Paper rustling in the sky
A gift is unwrapped

Quiet is the grass
Awaiting relief that comes
One drop at a time

The sky grinds his teeth
He unleashes a wild roar
His clouds churn with wrath

Ice rocks hit tin roofs
Ammunition from the sky
Rings through the air

The storm sings to me
A love song of cracks and booms
My favorite kind

Snowbound

I blink my eyes and shake my head
But darkness just won't go
The world looks dim and dingy
When I come in from the snow

My clumsy wayward footsteps
Are covered up and gone
Beneath the pure white blanket
That sparkles on my lawn

Snowflakes fill the sidewalk
Silence fills the air
Still, small voice calls out to me
I answer it with prayer

I'm positively snowbound
Frozen to my Lord
Blinded by the light of God
His warmth is my reward

Spring

As the heavy clouds lift from the winter sky
So also lifts the heaviness of my soul

As the sun shines forth and warms the cold ground
A newfound joy rises within and warms my spirit

As the faded blues and greens of the earth are renewed
The colors of my heart are reborn

The earth twirls giddily within the promise of spring
I share in its excitement

For God's appointed time is at hand, a time of new birth
Embrace the changes of the season and all God has in store

Sing with the birds of the air, thankful for the gift of today
While living in sweet anticipation of tomorrow's secret treasures

As a child eagerly waits for the dawn of Christmas morning
I will await spring

Inside

I'm not too much to look at
I've nothing great to say
In fact, my life seems sometimes
One long ordinary day

But feelings dwell within me
Deep down and out of reach
A hunger and fulfillment
Too complex to show or teach

The vessel may be tired
The body cracked and worn
But inside dwells a spirit
To testify that I'm reborn

So when you talk about me
Or condemn something I've done
Please remember my weak vessel
Can never live up to the Son

I know I am imperfect
That's obvious to see
But rest assured my Savior
Lives inside of me

Hands of Time

I marvel at the acrobatic hands
They bow and sweep and flow throughout the day
Never stopping to admire the work they've done
Unbeknownst to them if skies are blue or gray

The ever-faithful clock face holds them near
As they caress His never changing face
Within His perfect will there is no fear
Hands free to dance within His saving grace

I Am

As I live from day to day
Within God's will and in His ways
He does reveal to me the whole of
Who I am

There is so much more to me
Than just this body that you see
It is my soul inside that makes me
What I am

When I'm shaking where I stand
He extends His nail-scarred hand
Reminding me that in His grace is
Where I am

Even when I'm fast asleep
I know my heart and mind He'll keep
He is never tired and weak
When I am

As my life needs rearranging
My Father authors all the changing
He smiles, knowing the reason
Why I am

Tears

A precious gift
From creation to Creator
A thing of beauty

Flowing freely
Not balanced stubbornly on edge
Falling softly down

A sign of strength
The measure of a heart's greatness
From an eye once blind

Man is best reached
Through the wet and lonely pathway
Of a cleansing tear

Shells

I once was trapped inside a shell of inconsistency
My shell was hard, yet transparent; it cracked so easily

No way to beautify the surface, no seashell's perfect shine
My shell could not be tanned or worked like snakeskin left behind

Indeed my shell would crumble if a gust of wind blew strong
Before I came to Jesus Christ and saw clearly right from wrong

Look for me within the shadows of the woods, deep in the shade
Where the locust bursts forth from his shell and a new creature is made

You'll find me kneeling down below an old black locust tree
In search of shells—I will rejoice with each discovery

Nothing on the outside to be admired or sought
You have to search me from within, for with His love I'm bought

I am a brand new creature as clean as each new day
And with blessed assurance by His side I'll stay

Don't look for me upon the beach sifting through the sand
Collecting beautiful seashells for treasures in my hand

Look for me within the shadows of the woods, deep in the shade
Where the locust bursts forth from his shell and a new creature is made

You'll find me kneeling down below an old black locust tree
In search of shells—I will rejoice with each discovery

He Is There

The world swells with tears
Through the depths my God can tell
Which are mine

Savior of my soul
Traces their desperate flow
From my eyes

Such comfort to know
In the seas of dark despair
He is there

The Field

(Matthew 13:44)

I fought life's battles on my own
With neither sword nor shield
I feared my fall would end it all
Before I found the field

Quietly, I stumbled on
A treasure unrevealed
A fortune found within the ground
Led me to buy the field

Nothing saved—I sold my all
The deed was signed and sealed
I smiled inside, so satisfied
Because I bought the field

A buried treasure worth much more
Than earthly toil could yield
My very best was never blessed
Until I owned the field

Now I share the wealth I own
So others may be healed
Without delay, I'll join one day
The Master in His Field

Mighty Rushing Wind

Like rain, red flames pour from the sky
Into our thirsty souls
Crowns of fire surround our heads
From tongues strange language rolls

A rushing wind is all around
Streets echo with the roar
Curiosity abounds
Leading many to our door

Excitement they could not explain
They're drunkards, some men said
Though we are filled not with new wine
But with new hope, instead

The Holy Ghost has just arrived
To set us all on fire
Peter touched three thousand hearts
Through words God did inspire

Upsetting and unsettling
Such behavior does offend
Nothing shakes the shackles off
Like mighty rushing wind

Human Stone

A stone, a human building block, am I
Formed by the Rock the architects passed by

I serve a Rock that will not chain me down
Nor cast me in the mire to watch me drown

No shackles bind me; I am free to roam
His broad foundation, my tired feet call home

A solid Rock above the earth stands tall
The One who rules and reigns above us all

A stone, a useful human stone, am I
Conforming to this world, I dare not try

Stones of strength and courage line my sides
A church of human stones where faith resides

Stones in the world, but not stones of this earth
Shaped differently, but sharing one rebirth

As precious stones of beauty, we are prized
By God's own Cornerstone, Lord Jesus Christ

Speak Freely

When introduced to someone I've not met
I stumble looking for the words to say
Afraid I may say something I'll regret
When my self-conscious thoughts get in the way

Sometimes my voice will give a nervous shake
At times my eyes will travel to the ground
I think of all the new friends I could make
If only I'd relax and come unwound

But when I come before the God Most High
I never have to search for words to speak
My fears and worries travel from my tongue
Into the ears of One I often seek

He holds me in the comfort of His arms
Sometimes I cry as though my heart will break
This storm-filled world and its deceptive charms
Roll me away and crush me in their wake

But how my God does love to hear me talk!
He keeps His ear toward me, day and night
I never wonder if He'll scoff or balk
When words I form don't seem to come out right

Time rocks the cradle of my life on earth
My worldly cares shall fade as days grown dim
But God recalls the time of my rebirth
And all is well if I just speak with Him

Rise

Rise as the sun rises sure in the sky
Rise as the sparrow that never asks why

Rise and receive peace you can't understand
Rise as a thankful, true worshipful hand

Rise as prayers whispered to Heaven above
Rise to the rafters as praise filled with love

Rise from transgression; rise clean from your sin
Rise as the lame man God made walk again

Rise from fear's taunting; rise free from your doubt
Rise up like Lazarus when Christ said, "Come out!"

Rise and fall on Him; His burden is light
Rise soon to meet Him in heavenly flight

God Knows

Just as you know that a new day will dawn
Leaving soft morning dew glistening on your lawn

God knows your tomorrow

Just as your senses grasp seasons to come
The rosebud, the pumpkin, the sweet sugarplum

God knows your changes

Just as you know when nightfall is near
To shroud you for rest, or occasional tear

God knows your darkness

Just as you know things familiar to you
The special remembrance your heart holds onto

God knows your name

God knows your future, as He knows your past
You cannot outrun Him, no matter how fast
He gives peace eternal—the kind that will last

God knows you

King Of the Day

God of the morning, King of the day
Each moment, a gift I can never repay

With every new sunrise, You teach me to shine
Your breath of fresh air fills these dry lungs of mine

I stop and I read Your love letters at noon
Your bright midday sunlight makes jealous, the moon

For the moon can't compare to the warmth of the sun
Moonlight is hidden till daylight is done

You are the author of nightfall as well
You hear heart kept secrets that lips never tell

When the sun starts to fall and You say he must go
The moon is allowed then to lend us his glow

Father of morning of noon and of night
You make the wrong turns in this world turn out right

You guide and direct us with fingers unseen
Atonement is granted, our garments made clean

Your love for Your children cannot be denied
To love You or leave You—their choice to decide

But if they do love You, what joy it will bring
To live on this earth as a child of the King

Healing Hands

His thumbs caress the eyelids of the blind
His fingers smooth diseased and blistered skin
By His hands rough timber is refined
He holds the trembling hand withered in sin

With a wave the angry seas relax
His steady hand restrains the tossing ship
His sturdy palms support the weakest backs
An infant's fist curls on His fingertip

He wipes the tears of those who gently weep
His tender touch as peaceful as a dove
His hands break bread to feed His loyal sheep
His scars reveal the fullness of His love

What He's Not

We speak of our Lord Jesus
And all that He is, a lot
But let us take a moment
To reflect on what He's not

He's not a double-minded man
His words are clear and true
He's not uptight or selfish
For He gave His life for you

He's not one to hold grudges
He forgives each time He's asked
He's not idle or lazy
Providing help for others' tasks

He is not so quick to judge us
Tarries while we "get it right"
He is not forgetful of us
Brings a song in darkest night

He is not cut-down or mocked
Although the world may laugh and sneer
He will not withhold judgment
He will not fail to appear

He is not too small to heal our wounds
Or hear our faintest cries
He is not limited to our strength
He never is surprised

He does not wish our tongues to speak
Harshly of friend or foe
He will not withhold His blessings
From His children as they grow

Hero

He volunteered for duty

His uniform, the flesh of man

The stripes worn upon His body placed there not by ceremony

But by the strikes of a whip

His weapon: a two edged sword—the Word of Truth

I was a prisoner of unrighteousness

He fought diligently, on a rescue mission

That I might be set free from my captivity

His eyes remained upon me

As my own wandered with distraction

He was faithful

Even those who mocked Him could not escape His love

Betrayed by one He called friend

He was captured

He was wounded

He died

Allowing Himself to be murdered by the hands of men

That I might be saved by the grace of God

Three days in the grave

He arose

Leaving the finality of the tomb

To walk beside my unstable footsteps

He returned to the place of His death

Not to receive a medal of honor

But to receive me as His own

Unlocking my prison

He set me free

Continuing to lay Himself down as a bridge

He closes the gap for me

That I may come boldly before the throne of God

He asks only that I receive His gift, and love others

Never forgetting who rescued me from the darkness

Becoming salt and light that I may guide others

To everlasting life

Hold Your Breath

Do you find yourself too busy
With your cares from day to day?
How much would those cares be worth
If God took your breath away?

There's an easy way to find out
Just relax, breathe deeply in
In an instant you will realize
That you must breathe out again

Hold your breath and think of Jesus
Think of all His love and care
Focus on His home in Heaven
How He wants to meet you there

Hold your breath, remember Calvary
How your debt was fully paid
Hold your breath and thank Lord Jesus
For the sacrifice He made

Now your thoughts become united
As you thirst for precious air
The overwhelming need to breathe
Makes you forget your other cares

You forget about your problems
They just don't matter anymore
Now use your breath to praise Lord Jesus
After all, that's what it's for!

Use your breath to praise Lord Jesus
Praise Him for His daily care
Thank Him for His holy presence
That's worth so much more than air

Tell Him all of your shortcomings
What you want to rearrange
Seek ye first His lasting kingdom
Watch your life begin to change

Sweet Dreams

When much needed sleep eludes you
As you rest your weary head
In place of counting sheep tonight
Count blessings found instead

Remember all the miracles
When God supplied your grace
You'll soon be dreaming peacefully
A smile upon your face

Meditate upon His Word
He'll plant it in your heart
And then whenever darkness comes
Your faith won't fall apart

So when daylight turns to nightfall
And you find it hard to sleep
Don't forget to count your blessings
God will keep track of the sheep

Scrapbook

On the day of our birth
When arriving on this earth

I wonder if God takes a look
At His picture album book

He sees the finish from the start
Each skinned up knee and broken heart

Each milestone passed along the way
As auburn hair turns into gray

He sees us just as we shall be
When from this world we are set free

On our final earthly day
When time runs out for us to stay

Does He like how we fill in
The spaces between *now* and *then*...?

If blanks are filled with Christ inside
The Book of Life will open wide

True Love

Have you ever known a person
Who has prayed your soul to keep?
Who would still your stormy waters
When awakened from his sleep?

Have you ever met another
Who would bridge the gap for you?
Who would promise you forever
And then stay to see it through?

Has one given you a whisper
Spoken closely, soft and low?
Filled with wisdom and instruction
Guiding where you need to go?

Has the one that you hold dearly
Ever offered you his life?
Has he taken on your burdens
Stood beside you in your strife?

There is One who will not leave you
Or forsake you, come what may
He will gently mold and shape you,
Not give up and walk away

He will seat you at His table
The Living Water has been poured
Meet your true love and your Savior
He is Jesus Christ the Lord

Lady Truth

"That man is just and holy
I beg of you, don't let Him bleed
I have suffered in a dream for Him
And Jesus must be freed."

Such bitter, burden-laden tears
Your husband watched you cry
As he allowed the screaming crowd
Your King—to crucify

Blood is thicker than the water
Pilate dipped his hands within
Sorrow's brutal sobs escaped you
In mournful witness to his sin

Your newly opened eyes reveal
The vision you have seen
Tonight, sleep soundly knowing
Your true praying hands are clean

God's Odds

What are the odds of that?
What are the odds of this?
What are the odds that God ever worries
If odds are a *hit* or a *miss*?

Odds do not limit God's power
Nor should they hinder our trust
Beating the odds is the Lord's expertise
I should know, I was once made of dust

If the odds are not stacked in your favor
Lose not one moment of sleep
Against all the odds, it's not odd for our God
To cause lame men to jump up and leap

What are the odds He will love you?
And hold you when calm seas turn rough?
No odds to compare, you'll find that He's there
He died for you, oddly enough

First Place

Who said you were strong in the first place?
Who said you could conquer your fears?
Who said you could soar like an eagle?
Who said you could learn from your tears?

Who said you were loved in the first place?
Who said you would use self-control?
Who said you were fit for a temple?

The God who commissioned your soul.

Through

He reached out to me through a friend
Who encouraged me always to smile

Through my daughter's small generous hand
He convinced me pinecones are worthwhile

Through support from my spouse He has taught
There is healing through words that are kind

He reveals through the glass of my mirror
Earthly vessels become tired and lined

Through the confiding lips of my son
He has shown me the value of trust

Through mistakes I have made He reminds
Of my humble beginning from dust

His hands knead through every moment
Molding clay into what it should be

Through His will beats the heart of His promise
Bringing focus to all that I see

Little Men

My son stands up strong, and as brave as he can
Inside the gap somewhere between boy and man

How my heart weakens inside of my chest
When I tuck him in gently at nightfall to rest

I watch him now sleeping deep in the night
My eyes brim with tears that I can't seem to fight

Reaching under his pillow, I feel little men
Breathing sighs of relief I tiptoe out again

Little men guard the innocence of my child's heart
I take comfort in knowing toys still play a part

Within a boy's world, always moving so fast
Where the wide eyes of youthfulness don't seem to last

Lord, give me courage to face the day's dawn
When my fingers discover the little men gone

Experienced Tears

Thank You, Lord, for every time I did not win the race
For all those times I finished last with tears upon my face

I'm glad I was not chosen first to be on kickball teams
I'm thankful for a pounding heart that followed scary dreams

Thank You for each puppy lost, each bump, each bandaged knee
Every boy that made me cry, girls who looked down at me

I'm grateful for the hurtful words that cut me to the quick
I appreciate the times I cried when I was tired and sick

I thank You for the loneliness that chilled me to the bone
For every angry outburst, every fit I've ever thrown

Thank You Lord, for dead end roads, for loudly slamming doors
My children now can hear me say, "I have been there before"

They need my ears to listen and they need my guiding hand
The trying times within my life help me to understand

Growing up is difficult, I know their pain is real
I'm thankful I can comfort them by knowing how they feel

So thank You for allowing me to hang my head and cry
When faced with tiny broken hearts, I know the reason why

Live and Learn

Call me names, I'll shed a tear
You'll laugh and tell a friend
I'll learn how sharp a tongue can be
As my hurt feelings mend

Our differences are many
I'm sure you will agree
I will extract compassion
From the pain you've given me

I will not change my ways for you
God loves me, flaws and all
And if I see you stumble
I will try and break your fall

I thank you for the chance to feel
How deeply words can burn
I'll be a better comforter
To someone in return

Daddy, Why?

Daddy why does the sky only come in shades of blue?
And when I wish upon a star, why doesn't it come true?

And Daddy, why do rainbows always have to disappear?
Do you think we'd find a pot of gold if we could just get near?

Daddy, how do people make a baseball glove from leather?
And does Granny's elbow really ache before we get bad weather?

So many questions come so fast from such a little face
How can a father answer them with gentleness and grace?

Most of them I have no given answer for at all
Like, "Why does God decide to cause a shooting star to fall?"

I wonder if our Heavenly Father often perks His ear
And listens to the questions from the little men down here?

Of course, our God Almighty knows the ending from the start
The answers to our questions have been hidden in His heart

Like, "Why did husband run away," or "Why did loved one die?"
We have to hold onto the Lord, He knows the reason why

All things about this earth are not for us to know today
For in the twinkling of an eye it all will pass away

So try to trust the Father's will without a doubt or fear
And one day God will whisper precious answers in your ear

Ordinary Day

Today two golden rings unite a joyful bride and groom
Today a child was born into a waiting, sterile room

Today a family sobs and prays, fearing for a loved one's life
Today someone will harm a father's daughter or his wife

Today someone will marvel at a lifetime lived too fast
Today someone will realize this moment is his last

Today friendship will vanish when a push becomes a shove
Today a husband will turn from the wife he swore to love

Today someone will face the wall and cry tears of despair
Today someone will feel God's healing touch and tender care

Today someone will hear the greatest story ever told
Today someone will plant a seed and warm a heart grown cold

Today is ordinary, customarily arranged
Its significance known only to the hearts forever changed

Memories

We visit special people and relive a joyous day
Within our precious memory
Where our treasures hide away

We see Grandpa there with Grandma, smiling as they used to do
Back when air smelled somehow sweeter
And the sky seemed much more blue

We recall the words of wisdom whispered by departed friends
And we chuckle at jokes shared
Before the laughter had to end

When exciting news is breaking, we grab the phone to bend an ear
Then slowly hang up the receiver
Recalling they're no longer here

Weeds are growing in their gardens but their souls are blooming bright
An earthly home sits cold and empty
A heavenly mansion's filled with light

We sit visiting their memory while the choir voices sing
Loved ones claiming sweet Salvation
Already dining with the King

Take a moment to remember special loved ones that you miss
Recollect a happy smile
A warm embrace or tender kiss

Thank the Lord for precious memories—treasures buried day by day
Such a joy when we unearth them
After years have passed away

Bury many, filled with laughter, in the hearts of those you know
To be fondly excavated
When it comes your time to go

Pieces

When working on a puzzle, anticipation grows
Although you hold a crucial piece, you're unsure where it goes

Life remains a puzzle that only God has solved
He knows before conflict begins, how it will be resolved

Within your deep uncertainty God's perfect will is found
The light of sheer excitement shines where darkness did abound

What a thrill to know you're covered by His mercy and His grace
To gently fit the piece you hold into His waiting space

Exhilaration fills you as your piece slips in just right
Lay before Him all life's pieces; a seeking heart is His delight

Mercy

With mercy renewed every morning
He stands with His arms open wide
He knows when I let sin entice me
He unveils what my soul tries to hide

From God there exists not one secret
I was His before the world turned
Often I feel so defeated
I've forgotten the lessons I've learned

For God is the mighty schoolmaster
I must study before I can rest
Lest I become weak and weary
Unable to pass life's great test

God help me break through this resentment
It burns me right down to my bones
Remind me of Your gentle mercy
Assure me I'm never alone

For Your love is pure joy beyond measure
Your peace is unlike the world gives
And I know when I seek I will find You
For within me Your spirit does live

Water Under the Bridge

Many times we've hurt each other, first one thing and then another
Our burning anger ravishing our minds.

Ruled by our intense emotion, crashing waves just like the ocean
Lashing out, we feel so justified.

Crossing bridges ripe for burning as thoughts of rage continue turning
We throw matches right into our gasoline.

Only to find the bridges mended, not black with ash as we intended
In disbelief we test the platforms once again.

Who do you think does the mending and stands within the gap defending
All the bridges that we try so hard to burn?

As the fire inside us rages, who is the One that turns the pages
In the book of ever-after that we share?

I'm so thankful that the Living Water flows and is forgiving
As it makes its way beneath our burning bridge.

Living Water does replenish and ensures we won't diminish
As we press on to revive and to rebuild.

All we are is never lost because our Savior paid the cost
He's in the water underneath the burning bridge.

May we learn to walk together over bridges and forever
Call upon the Carpenter with all our hearts.

And when embers start rekindling on the bridges You are mending
Let conviction fall upon our troubled brows.

Let us not be such slow learners, make us menders and not burners
As we honor every oath in love we vow.

Love Is

Angry flames consume me whole
Hot tears swell my eyes
Justified

Your finger taps my shoulder
My heart is rabid
Filled with rage

You remind me of Your Word
Resistance is thin
Fury calms

Love is patient; Love is kind
Love is not selfish
As I am

Oh, thank You Holy Spirit
Once more You bring sight
To the blind

Night Whisper

Puffed up and proud
My thoughts are loud
I toss and turn in bed

I make things worse
Inwardly curse
Pass judgment in my head

I close my eyes
I feel so wise
My anger's justified

But as I doze
My spirit knows
A war wages inside

He whispers soft
As I drift off
Still voice as sweet as song

And when I wake
My heart does ache
Forgive me, I was wrong

Bygones

A longing churns within my soul
A hunger unfulfilled
I smash the crystal hourglass
The sands of time are spilled

I dip my toes into the sand
My eyes begin to burn
I wipe a hot escaping tear
As memories return

I try to drag them back with me
Into the here and now
But they embody youthfulness
And I've forgotten how

I used to measure happiness
By counting every kiss
Collecting pictures in my mind
For such a time as this

But as my thoughts seek treasure deep
Within the mounting sand
My soul is busy stringing pearls
Unearthed by Wisdom's hand

Wish

My son peered upon me, curiously
"If you could have one wish, what would it be?"
I thought a moment, searching in my mind
No extraordinary needs there did I find
After much consideration I did speak
But changed my mind about the wish I'd seek

"Well, son, I'd like to wish good health to stay
But what if God allows illness one day
As a means to teach us something we should know
Why wish gone His desire to watch us grow?
And if I wish for much financial gain
I might become self-satisfied and vain
A wish for youth and never to grow old
Would rob me of the wisdom God foretold
Could wishing for sure comfort all my days
Restrict my faith and empathetic ways?"

I began to think of strain within my life
Time limits, stressful job, internal strife
If given opportunity to choose
I just can't help but think I'd somehow lose
If I could up and wish it all away
There'd be no reason left for me to pray

"My son, I know it's fun to wish and dream
But remember things aren't always as they seem
Opportunity for growth, disguised as pain
A chance to call the Savior's name again
When everything is well within your soul
Let the virtue of contentment be your goal."

Millstone

Afraid to leave her alone at the swing
Terror grips at my heart, yet I still cling
To a world that appalls me—humans ugly and mean

And forgiveness I can't bear to find
For the killer and all of his kind
Wrenching images course through my mind

My breath gets caught in my chest
I imagine her mother's unrest
Surviving the ultimate test

God, rescue my soul as You turn
From within me this anger that burns
With a feverish hatred discerned

The children don't want us to hate
But to love, and to patiently wait
For our appointed reunion date

While they nap in the arms of the King
And clap as the angel choir sings
They've forgotten the pain others bring

The Moment

You plan your trip so carefully
Packed bags hold dreams inside
No destination guaranteed
Find joy within the ride

While rushing by you barely see
The street you're running through
No guarantee you'll make it home
So smell a rose or two

The future, known to God alone
Is hidden from your sight
You may not see the evening stars
Or view the morning light

One single moment at a time
Is all God will allow
Within this disappearing mist
Enjoy the here and now

Thank God

Life happens in small doses
Our God planned it all that way
And things never run as smoothly
As we'd like them to each day

If your child is filled with mischief
It seems you always have to scold
Hug him tight and thank Lord Jesus
For giving you a child to hold

Our lives are oh-so-busy
Interruptions never cease
If we learn how to embrace them
We attain internal peace

You're busy when a neighbor calls
Your ear she hopes you'll lend
Listen up attentively
Thank God you have a friend

No one knows your heart
Quite like the Lord does—this is true
But it soothes the soul to share
Your inside heart with others too

At times your spouse unnerves you
In ways you just can't understand
Thank God you have a partner
To walk through life with, hand in hand

How many tests we face each day
Some passed, some failed by far
I'm thankful that our Savior
Loves us just the way we are

Sketching Tomorrow

Take no day for granted
Not morning sun, nor moon
Uncharted winds are blowing
And change is coming soon

Hold hands longer and harder
Hold gazes, thoughts, and smiles
Hold no trace of bitterness
Or judgment that defiles

Love without conditions
With no guarantee
Commit without resistance
Trust, but not foresee

Indeed the road is turning
But Christ stands at the end
Author, finisher of faith
Beginning and the end

A stronghold in your troubles
A fountain in your drought
A shoulder where your head can rest
When tears are all cried out

The sketch of my tomorrow
A faint and unclear line
Achieving focus when I pray
Lord, not my will, but Thine

Things

The things my life consists of
That mean so much to me
Will not be here much longer
No earthly thing will be

Violently I hold on
To things that come and go
Instead of finding comfort
Within the God I know

Yet I just keep clinging
To things I hold as dear
Begging God to promise
To always keep them near

The earth is temporary
And all that spins within
No promise of forever
For all good things must end

God speaks peace unto me
Reminding me what's real
I can't take things to Heaven
But I can take what I feel

The things of most importance
All the love I have inside
The secrets that my heart knows
My soul, where dreams reside

The only things that matter
Are things that change the heart
Such changes I'll take with me
To my heavenly new start

Life Under Glass

Some memories grow sweeter
With time, it seems to me
But sugary delusions
Soon lose their validity

In truth, life happens here and now
Alive in present tense
Life ebbs and flows, it dims and glows
Not always making sense

I capture life in pen and ink
With photographs and paint
But colors find it hard to breathe
Under constant restraint

Captured life is hindered
As a butterfly contained
True beauty is not realized
When wings fold up—restrained

Life is like a butterfly
Beauty revealed in flight
No human hand can captivate
The soul's true inner light

Little Things

God plucks a petal daily
From the flower each life brings
Many petals have grown withered
Thirsting for the little things

Gentle whispers, soft caresses
A tender kiss from lips that sing
Human hearts grow cold and empty
Without the warmth of little things

Hearts too weak to hold one problem
And the heaviness it brings
Open up and find the strength
To carry countless little things

Words like ointment, softly spoken
Into open wounds that sting
Can bring healing beyond measure
Words are wondrous little things

Children cry and reach out for us
In the darkness this world brings
Oh Lord guide us in the handling
Of Your precious Little Things

Promise?

If life on earth is fragile
Why do we still suppose
Tomorrow is a promise
From which our future grows?

Tomorrow is no promise
Our future starts today
So hold hands with your Savior
And let Him lead your way

Just because this world is turning
Doesn't mean it always will
One day God might rebuke it
And cause it to stand still

Perhaps the passing seasons
Are ordered not to change
Or God decides to shuffle
And have them rearrange

Maybe God will blow the stars out
Like candles in the wind
And the lonely moon won't dare to light
Our darkest night again

What would happen to the prospect
Of our precious dreams and plans?
Would we then admit our future
Rests within the Master's hands?

All In a Day's Grace

To rise, to fall, to risk it all, what do You have in store?
Will You put someone in my path, or lead one to my door?

To stay at home, or go outside, what plans have You for me?
Surround me with new faces or familiarity?

My "to do" list sits before me; will I check chores neatly off?
Or will You write a new list to ensure my heart stays soft?

I find it hard, relinquishing control over my day
Ever gently, You remind me, time is not mine anyway

Help me not to be disheartened if You wish to change my plan
Stretch my arms beyond presumption to extend Your mighty hand

Come Quickly

God's promises are many
Life's certainties are few
Painted by the hands of time
My portrait, sad but true

As destined is the sun to rise
And fall within the sky
So is the constant way of man
To live, and then to die

But how to bear the in between,
This dreadful hanging on?
The rise and fall of hollow chest
When will has traveled on

With God forever on my lips,
Unceasingly I pray
Pull me from this trap of flesh
Into Your arms today

But if relief from labored breath
Is not this day designed
Let me endure the hours ahead
With quiet peace of mind

Cheap Tricks

Illusion is his claim to fame

To trick the eye

To blur the line between good and evil

To disguise the darkness in the attire of light

Not by dramatic transformation

But with subtle movement

A trace of shade and shadow

He hopes you won't notice his sleight of hand

Sometimes you don't

His smoke and mirrors go undetected

It was so in the garden

An ear perked up by reason

An eye blurred by greed

He mused over what little effort it took

To steal, kill, and destroy

But he is no match for our God

No tricks, no optical illusion

In the garden, or in the wilderness

Only truth, straightforward and bold

Evil is sent slithering back to the darkness

From which it emerged

But even the darkness shines as day

To our God

Thorns

Jesus told a story
Of the sower and his seed
Some fell along the wayside
And the birds began to feed

Some landed on the stony ground
No earth to hold them in
Seeds that sprang up quickly
Scorched and withered in the end

Some seeds were sown among the thorns
Which choked their tender sprouts
Plants designed for bearing fruit
Would forever be without

I'm so afraid I'll lose my way
And fall among the thorns
The thorns of life distract me
From the fact that I'm reborn

I pray that I will recognize
The thorns upon my path
And be strong enough to pull free
From the thorns of pride and wrath

I long to weed the thorns away
And grow in godly ground
To be the seed sown in good soil
With fruit to weigh me down

Unblink

Time is an impatient child running down a busy street
She tightly grips me by the hand
Jostling, jarring, whipping in the wind
A voiceless smile stitched to my ragdoll face
Red painted cheeks
Wide unblinking eyes plead…
Slow down

Fearless

Fear is smoke and mirrors
Illusion at its best
An overestimated trick
Designed to cause unrest

Though fear seeks to harm me
It will not steal my peace
When outwardly I tremble
My soul will rest at ease

I may shake for a moment
I may break down and cry
But fear is temporary
My tears will soon be dry

The peace I've found in Jesus
Is not the worldly kind
Transcending understanding
It guards my heart and mind

Sprinkle

Under sunless skies
Led by invisible strings
Flowers dance

A single leaf waves
Petals bow down and spring up
Soft shower

My foolish heart fears
His mercy falls down like rain
Gentle Lord

A Thread

Suspended over fiery pits
Above the hungry sea
My dangling feet entice the jaws
That would devour me

I hear the wails of anguish
I breathe the stench-filled air
I know what lies beneath me
To look down, I couldn't dare

Above the Wicked Weaver's loom
I'm hanging by a thread
His tapestry, not formed of cloth
But woven souls instead

Chin and eyes held upward
I tightly hold my grip
From my lips a whispered prayer
"Dear God, don't let me slip"

This thread I tightly cling to
Is no ordinary string
But a gently woven lifeline
From the garment of the King

My thread cannot be broken
Or singed by Satan's flame
So I'll keep hanging by a thread
Secure, in Jesus' name

No Doubt

Perfecting work within me
With mercy flowing deep
Forsaking not, works of Your hand
Your promise is to keep

Knowing when I lay to rest
Watching as I rise
Helping me to shed each day
The scales that close my eyes

The night is dark and without sound
In fear, my thoughts do run
For You the depths of blackest night
Shine as the noonday sun

You are strong within my weakness
You are love when I'm without
You clear confusion from my mind
In You, I have no doubt

Believe

My feet are shaky and unsure
My thoughts seem cloudy and obscure

I'm not sure what to do or say
I let my fears confuse the way

Influence lies on either side
Concerns of worldly, wounded pride

A peculiar people, most would agree
Seems scarier when there's only me

No brothers or sisters to strengthen my word
But then I remember the voices I've heard

"Not by might, nor by power"
My spirit is strong, I will not cower

I will arise, and I will speak
Stand true to God's Word, yet be gentle and meek

I will ask for His guidance, and I will receive
For He gives life eternal to all who believe

Time

Time, you march on
Marching over us all
At neck-breaking speed
Or at heartbreaking crawl

Shall I be your master
And hold back your hands?
Forcing submission
Shouting demands?

Or shall I breathe deeply
As you have your way
Hammering, chiseling
Sculpting each day

Transforming an enemy
Into a friend
Giving the hopeless
A dream to defend

Healing the wounds
In the body and mind
Returning our sight
When the world robs us blind

Helping a sinner
Emerge as a saint
Marching in freedom
Time fears no restraint

Little Foxes

Oh, you little foxes!
Scampering the earth
Nipping us with tiny teeth
The moment of our birth

Your tails are full and bushy
Your eyes are bright and clear
Enticement fills the vineyard gates
Whenever you are near

But, oh, you ugly foxes!
Within your pelts of red
A heartbeat thumps but no blood pumps
Pure poison flows instead

The poison of distraction
The bitter pill of haste
Destroying tender vines of grapes
Our lips have yet to taste

Oh, you clever foxes!
Too many to keep track
You run with our attentiveness
Never looking back

You light your tails on fire
And swing them as a sword
Burning up the sweet first-fruits
We've promised to our Lord

Woe to you, poor foxes
Unto this world you cling
The feeding hand you long to bite
Belongs to Christ our King

So you just run along now
On prayer we'll concentrate
A fox stands little chance against
The God we supplicate

Song in the Darkness

While it is yet dark
Birds sing outside my window
Anticipating the coming dawn
With light-filled voices

The world is black
My hands shake in the shadows
Peeking through the blinds
I dare not speak

Boldly, the wise birds sing
Faith inhabits their song
Soon dawn will break
Spilling light onto the treetops

I sit in silence
Doubting the light
Shuddering in the weak glow
Of my own candle

Still the birds sing
Bestowing a song upon the rising sun
A melody written in darkness
A gift of thanks for the light to come

Sight Unseen

Jesus let me thrust my hand
Into Your side once more
Let me feel the empty scars
Where nails pierced through before

Whispered fears burn in my ears
My soul I can't defend
The doubts I feel, do linger still
Like ashes on the wind

I must see with my own eyes
The prints upon Your hands
But I have no authority
To make such high demands

Oh, Holy Spirit Comforter
Turn darkness into light
Walk me down the path of trust
By faith and not by sight

Fatherly

Did You lean forward on Your throne to witness my first step?
In childhood long to comfort me and hold me as I wept?

Did Your heart swell inside You when I clung to the right choice?
Did disappointment find You when I disobeyed Your voice?

Did You hold high hopes for me when I had no hope at all?
Could You discover faith in me the times I feared a fall?

You've always seen the best in me—I know You see it still
I feel Your fatherly embrace when I seek first Your will

Roots

I gaze upon the rose bush, beauty beyond compare
I enjoy its sweet aroma that lingers in the air

I admire the vivid colors appearing on its blooms
I hold a high respect for thorns (you know why, I presume)

Although each part is special, the one held close by me
Is the ugly, gnarled, and twisted part, the part I cannot see

Buried deep within the darkness, never warming in the sun
The roots hold up God's masterpiece—their work is never done

Unlike the ever changing rose whose blossoms come and go
The roots hold fast with all they have and make the branches grow

Beauty is illusive, it abandons in the end
For holding firm to shaky ground on roots I will depend

Playing in the Weeds

I've fallen in the thorns again
Old wounds begin to bleed
I came to pick a flower
Just to find it was a weed

Strangled and entangled by
The brambles on the ground
Pulled so deeply into earth
I fear I won't be found

I claw with dirty fingernails
My knuckles cracked and split
Helplessly I pray the Lord
To free me from this pit

He excavates me once again
And washes off my hands
Tenderly, He cleans my wounds
With love, He reprimands

Father, keep me close to home
Far from the tares that snare
Your grass is always greenest
When my eyes are closed in prayer

Let me not be tempted
Beyond Your garden place
Where mercy grows in endless rows
Beside Your streams of grace

Make Believe

My toys are scattered out upon the lawn
So hard I've played, enjoying every role
Sometimes good-guy, sometimes villain-cruel
To spend each day pretending is my goal

From sunup to sundown it's hide and seek
Or freeze-tag with my friends from down the lane
Red light-Green light is delightful fun
A heart possessed by pleasure feels no pain

But hunger's rumble will not be denied
Relentless is the soul's persistent churn
It strikes as I skip through the midday sun
Emptiness, like fire, does hotly burn

Shadows fall, now time to come inside
My toys lay scattered, broken all around
Within the dark I grope for helping hands
Around me not one playmate can be found

My lip begins to tremble in the night
When make believe and costumes fall away
I can't pretend when I am all alone
To God the nighttime shines as bright as day

Child's Play

I am like a little child
Preparing for a duel
I cushion, pad and quilt myself
(Child's play can be so cruel)

I strap those puffy pillows on
With Daddy's biggest belt
And soon the nudges of a blade
Are barely even felt

No sword can penetrate my heart
So warm and snug within
Its muffled beats are heavy
With my un-repented sin

I hold my breath and shut my eyes
I swing my sword of wood
I slice the air to ribbons
But it doesn't do much good

The Lord will cut right through the fluff
And pierce my thin façade
His blade is double-edged and quick
The Living Word of God

Daydream

Tender blades of grass grew sweet
They tickled under childish feet
Small hands that grass stains lingered on
Cartwheeled happily on the lawn

On summer grass I'd lay and dream
Pretending clouds weren't as they seem
At times a ship would billow by
Or wild, white horses rode the sky

Sweet scents of autumn filled the air
Leaves clothed the grass and trees were bare
I'd roll across the patchwork lot
Lost in a land that time forgot

Winter grass glistened cold and hard
A garden of jewels replaced our yard
Bundled up tight I'd run and play
A wonderland far from dreary days

I look back now on yesteryear
I seemed immune to pain and fear
In a world composed of fenced-in grass
Where grownups never dared to pass

I miss that world so far from now
Daydreams grow dark with age somehow
My heart changed playing grownup games
But the heart of Christ remains the same

Now He's that fortress where I run
Where letting go can still be fun
A childlike faith is safe with Him
He brightens as the world turns dim

Unlike the clouds that disappear
God's outline is forever clear
No fear from shadows, dark and strange
God stays the same when seasons change

Grow Up

Shouting for attention, yet afraid to stand alone
We call ourselves adults now, but we haven't fully grown

"Watch me, Daddy, watch me!" from daring heights we call
But when we stumble down we scream, "Don't look at me at all!"

We stiffen with defiance while tears sting in our eyes
Resentful of the times we must resist temptation's cries

We measure our own worthiness by other men's success
True, we are God's children, but we're spoiled none the less

Bit by bit our selfish pride grows fatter day by day
While inside our hungry souls are wasting fast away

The Path

Your still, small voice

Seems to shout my name

I wake from my slumber

At odds with peace

Restless in spirit

Knowing I have strayed Your path

I haven't gone far

I am on the shoulder

At the edge of the trail

Picking wildflowers

But the bouquet I arrange

Is only one of weeds

Without the Master's touch

You call out to me

Calling me back

To where the path is still straight

Where the flowers grow most vibrant

Not along the side of the path

But at the end

For Sale, Like New

I stopped by a rummage sale just the other day
I've such a fascination with the things men sell away

I saw a pair of sandals with sand upon the soles
The owner must have walked a lot, to wear so many holes

I also saw a basin, once used for washing feet
Beside it lay an apron, now folded nice and neat

A crown, twisted and thorny, had three nails tucked inside
Remnants of past suffering, when Christ was crucified

Standing tall against the sky a wooden cross remained
For sale on special discount—old, rugged, and blood-stained

Once the seller gave his word, but he withheld his heart
Too many burdens on his back to play the "Christian part"

"It's not too late!" I shouted, and ran to tell him why
But lost him in the growing crowd of folks eager to buy

Give Christ your heart completely, trust Him and take a stand
His gift of life-eternal is never secondhand

Say Cheese

Mothers often tell their children
When lightening throws a spark or two
"God is just taking your picture"
But what if those words were true?

What if God designed a camera
That could zoom in on your day
Taking photographs at random
To hang in Heaven for display?

Would His lens find strength and beauty
In the child He caught off guard
Planting seeds in souls of others
Tenderizing hearts grown hard?

Or has the world become your focus
With its power to distract
Would the God-sized shutter click
Without your dignity intact?

Would God's camera find you sharing
Peaceful words of love and grace
Or would stress and irritation
Be expressed upon your face?

God's mighty eye is fixed within you
Snapping pictures of your mind
Flashing light into dark places
Exposing thoughts of every kind

So don't wait for strikes of lightening
To confirm God's watching you
His photo album spans your lifetime
Each page open for review

The Reading of His Will

In God's book I'm living
To serve the One I love
And every puzzle piece of life
Slips in like hand and glove

In God's book I'm humble
And meek in every way
I see the pain behind the masks
For enemies, I pray

In God's book I'm quiet
And practice self-control
My lips await the fiery touch
From God's anointed coal

In God's book I'm serving
I work with all my might
Leading other souls to Christ
And standing for what's right

In God's book I follow
His Spirit and His creed
My life perfected by His will
…If I would only read

Dust

Dust you were; dust you will be
Only in My love will you ever be free

The hairs on your head, I have numbered each one
I brought you Salvation through the death of My son

I have knocked; I have waited; I have called you by name
You have run, and you've hidden, and caused yourself shame

I provide you with blessings, each day something new
But you only seek heartache; what more can I do?

If you drink not the water to which you've been led
You'll thirst for the cup of destruction instead

So choose you this day who to serve—call on Me
And when dust claims your body, your soul will be free

Strength

Samson, set apart by God, so set apart am I
Accomplishing His sovereign will, not always knowing why

As the Angel of the Lord ascended in the flame
My soul takes flight above my flesh, never to be the same

Each day reflects a plan of God, for the captive and the free
I know from where my strength is drawn—God's spirit stirs in me

Lion-maiming power with a taste for something sweet
My tongue has flair for riddles, landing me in dark deceit

But even when I'm bound without, freedom resides within
Grace to face the enemy, forgiveness from my sin

At times I lose my focus and offer up my hair
Only to find I'm grinding, blind, in a temple of despair

Lord, remember me, O God, and strengthen me once more
To crush my millstone, dense with pride, to dust upon the floor

Gold

Pure gold waits up in Heaven
But I have gold on earth
Too much to put a price upon
Or estimate the worth

With golden opportunities
I'm greeted every day
And silent golden moments shine
To clear dark clouds away

Throw in a golden sunset
And a golden rule or two
To paint a golden portrait of
My life, so blessed by You

God help me to remember You
My first priority
Lest I create an idol from
This gold You've given me

Wasted Beauty

As I sit alone
I look over my shoulder
I see a river deep
Quiet beauty
Cool and calm
Green grass and noble trees line the banks
A turtle swims slowly upon the surface of the water
A small footbridge crosses over in the shade
I long to stand on that bridge
I long to gaze down upon the water

I walk toward the river
I near the green banks
I step onto the footbridge
I see the turtle swimming slowly by
I look around me, above and below
I do not think about the cool air
I do not think about this single moment in time
A precious gift from God

I think of who is watching me
I think of menial chores ahead
I think of things to be purchased at the market
I think of the job awaiting me
I think of things that I should do differently
I think of yesterday's regrets

The moment slips by
I must leave now
Satan laughs at me softly
On this beautiful summer morning

What Kind

When I am kind to others and offer them a smile
Is it because I value them and feel they are worthwhile?

Or is it obligation that draws the niceness out?
Just grit my teeth and bear it, holding back the urge to shout

Perhaps it's utter selfishness that makes me smile and nod
To agree with other points of view while wearing my façade

I just want them to like me, reputation I must save
I have to go the extra mile and never make a wave

But what glory has my Father if I'm always *saving face*?
Thriving on the world's approval, not depending on God's grace?

Kindness reflects the Savior, arms wide open, all the way
Lord, help me lose myself and share Your kind of love today

Tug of War

I have a tug of war each day within my point of view
What will they think if I don't/What will You think if I do?

Take sides with the underdog; stand up when others won't
What will they think if I do/What will You think if I don't?

Laugh the longest and the loudest, make fun of others when it's true
What will they think if I don't/What will You think if I do?

Remember people's errors, put every word they've said, "in quotes"
What will You think if I do/What will they think if I don't ?

To love the most unlovable, turn cheek when hate burns through
What will You think if I don't/What will they think if I do?

Rejoice in my Salvation, share the Word of Life You wrote
What will they think if I do/Will they perish if I don't?

What they think cannot compare to the joy that will shine through
When I stand for what is right because my Father told me to

The Screen

When I heard You knocking, my door opened wide
Greeting You humbly, I asked You inside
You rearranged furniture; I swept the place clean
But today I realized I closed back the screen

The screen door is filtering all that comes in
Holiness will not cross the doorstep of sin
Screening my spirit and questioning why
Blocking the entrance as You're walking by

I used to rise early to study Your Word
Now the shrill sound of my snooze alarm's heard
I leave my door open—but now there's a catch
Convenience is key to my front screen door's latch

My threshold grows cold though my Savior's in sight
The screen door has filtered out God's warmth and light
Deep down inside my soul longs to be seen
I leave my door open, and unhinge the screen

Receiver

My receiver must be broken
Or my wires are wearing thin
I can talk to God for hours
But hear nothing coming in

I just jabber, chit and chatter
Telling Him about my day
Remind Him of my busy schedule
Let Him know that I'm okay

Then I run to obligation
Jump through hoops and volunteer
I almost always halfway listen
For that voice I used to hear

I forget now how it sounded
I think it whispered small and still
It's the voice that used to guide me
And direct me to God's will

All my wires are crossing lately
And there's static on the line
Shouting voices screaming at me
I pretend that all is fine

It's much too loud to hear a whisper
I'm far too busy to kneel down
My head and heart have both grown weary
My spirit groans without a sound

Agenda fills while faith grows empty
Soon there's none left to defend
Long neglected Holy Spirit
Receive that still, small voice again

Inside Out

Doctor, I need an operation
Something's wrong, I have no doubt
I've noticed lately that my "in"
Doesn't match up with my "out"

What I'm feeling on the inside
When a favor's asked of me
Is sometimes anger or resentment
That I won't let others see

On the outside I am gracious
Meek and gentle as a dove
But my heart is filled with discord
Not with mercy or with love

Can you help me today, Doctor?
See, I want both parts to match
I want to serve my neighbor wholly
Without selfish strings attached

I want arms that open fully
And a heart that's open too
I want a voice that offers comfort
And a smile that's warm and true

Self-absorption is the culprit
Could you cut it to the quick?
Please replace it with compassion
A bit of grace should do the trick

I know surgery is risky
But I'll gladly bear the pain
If it means a heart that's humble
And a conscience clear again

I need to show my loved ones
What God's love is all about
But I'll testify in vain
Until my insides match my out

Expectation

Another day, unable to meet expectations
Good intentions, spread too thin
A smile, a wink
A false sense of security
A mental blame blanketed over others
I hold myself back
A new day ahead
Will I ever arrive to the place
Where no regrets lie?
Will I ever get it right?
Things were easier before light was shed
When an excuse could be made
Before my skin was transparent
In that time, before the truth arrived
My hands appeared clean before my eyes
As well as the eyes of others
Inside, an unclean soul hung
Black as night
Away from consciousness
Away from awareness
The fear came only now and again
What will become of me when I die?
I now behold the beauty of truth
All things pale in comparison
My walk is not easy, the falls are inevitable
The recovery is painful and sometimes slow
But every step is worth so much
One step closer to the perfection of my Father
A time when the emptiness of earthly expectations
Will be replaced with never ending peace

Have Cross, Will Carry

When I took the cross upon me, it didn't seem so hard to bear
It didn't seem so inconvenient, it caused no worry or despair

But the cross grew far too heavy as I traveled down the road
Became a hassle and a bother, a cumbersome and bulky load

Pretty soon I found it easy just to lay the cross aside
Lean it up against the doorway, instead of dragging it inside

I'd force it in the car each morning, and leave it in the parking lot
And in the hustle of my day, not give the cross a second thought

But in the long dark hour of midnight—when my heart began to race
How I needed God, my Father, but I feared His angry face

I was ashamed of my behavior, how I longed to make things right
Then I realized I'd forgotten where I left the cross that night

For the only way to God is through His one and only son
The man who took my sins upon Him, and on the cross, Salvation won

But how could I attempt to reach Him? I felt my cause a total loss
Until I stumbled on my pride and fell down on the rugged cross

I wrapped my trembling arms around it, kneeling there on bended knee
Sobbing openly, repentant of the sin revealed in me

In an instant came His comfort, a tender voice spoke soft and low
"That cross was carried on My body; My back is stronger than you know

Devote your time to Me, your Savior, don't lean My cross upon the wall
And when it gets too hard to carry, all you have to do is call."

Choosing to Hear

Still voice, are You still calling underneath a sky that's falling?
Your voice so small and calm amidst the craze
Am I the one too busy to ask myself, "Where is He?"
When I haven't heard a word from You in days?

Could it be I am so caught up, drinking nectar from the world's cup
That I neglect to listen for the sound
Of the voice that I know can, save the blackened soul of man
By calling for the lost until they're found?

How Your words did ring so true as I made the time for You
Your voice would usher in the peace of God
Now it seems my ears are blocked and under chains my heart is locked
My spirit and my mind at constant odds

Still, small, voice, please keep on calling and I'll try to keep from falling
As I stumble on this road along the way
Sometimes all that keeps me going is the hope that comes with knowing
I will meet the voice's Master some sweet day

A Moment's Peace

My moments buzz with activity
A heavy droning sound
That hurts my ears
And hangs my head

I stretch each moment over my skin
Sides splitting, seams bursting
Pouring myself into time
To avoid pouring myself out to God

Distracting myself
From the quiet moments spent in His presence
The refreshment to my soul
The sweetening of my tongue

His moments sing with crystal clarity
A light and joyful song
That tickles my ears
And lifts my chin

Choosing to hear
Blaring babble
Over soft stillness
I hang my head

Weaving

I can hear the skillful clicking
Of his fervent needles knitting
As he weaves his swiftly flowing web of lies

Exquisite stitching does impress me
As his silky threads caress me
The world around me alters right before my eyes

Innocence loses its glisten
As my curious ears listen
To the dark tapestry woven all around

Threads I once considered golden
Become weak and soon are broken
When compared with this embroidery I've found

Stitching frantically in rhythm
Weaving all I have, and then some
Spinning round I find my heartstrings wound in knots

Tightly holding onto thread ends
I let go, revealing dead ends
In darkness I recall the light I once forgot

Ornate threads still seek to hold me
Tempting, tormenting the old me
But I walk through every web without a snare

For a new me stands before you
With a never seen before view
Now I leave my weaving in the Father's care

First Fruit

The fruit, alive with color
Promises more to come
I'll harvest in the morning
Such work is wearisome

My labor is rewarded
Good soil has passed the test
Time to lay my toil aside
And give my bones a rest

At midnight as I slumber
God rouses me from sleep
Reminding me to offer Him
The fruit I'd hoped to keep

I'll rise in early morning
Give the first fruit of my day
Instead of giving what is left
When time has had its way

Before I feed my body
My spirit must be fed
I'll drink sweet solitude as wine
God's Word will be my bread

I offer You my morning light
You quench my daily thirst
Lord, thank You for reminding me
To set Your table first

Unresolved

Restlessness plagues me—my body and soul
My mind and heart race wildly out of control

I toss and I turn, raging deep in the night
A sad chord strikes through me, my life is not right

My brow frowns and furrows, I want no one's touch
I never knew small sins could weigh quite so much

I think of the unrest that dwells in Hell's flame
The unresolved feelings of guilt and of shame

Should I trade Salvation for sin's worthless snare?
Is burning eternal a fate I could bear?

Break me with conviction, my face to the ground
With tears I will thank You; repentance I've found

Under the Rug

Oops, not again, a *little sin* to sweep under the rug
"Everybody makes mistakes," I tell myself, and shrug

The tiny pile of hidden dirt grows bigger day by day
And soon the rug cannot conceal the mountainous display

I trip upon the mound and fall each morning when I rise
It doesn't vanish in the night, much to my own surprise

It causes such distraction when I kneel down in prayer
For as I speak to God I feel its shadow looming there

What happened to the little smudge of dust I swept aside?
A rising mountain grows from all the little sins I hide

Should I fall down upon the Rock that sets my conscience free?
For if by choice I hesitate, the Rock shall fall on me

Tin Man

I feel just like the Tin Man
Stiff and filled with rust
My heart is in there, somewhere
But it's covered up with dust

My dull eyes stare out blankly
They take the world right in
Adjusting to the darkness
Barely blinking at the sin

With one leg frozen solid
On each side of the fence
It seems I have forgotten
My mind's true residence

My conscience starts to crumble
An eroding, empty hole
No oil can in my future now
Corrosion floods my soul

Restless

Is sin a shrouded secret?
Or the unrest that it brings?
Preoccupation of the mind
Distracts from godly things

The gentle turning of the head
The drawing of the eye
The cunning voice that whispers low
It never hurts to try

Thus begins the hiding
The duck and cover game
The running from the will of God
The unrelenting shame

My little box of secrets is
An open book to God
My smile, a transparent disguise
Predictable façade

The secrets that so thrill my heart
Contaminate my soul
Self-righteously, I tell myself
That *I* am in control

But how my God knows differently!
Control is not my own
My righteousness is filthy rags
Unfit before the Throne

Snake Handler

Twisting through my burdened mind
Dark thoughts slip up from behind
Self-righteous venom seeps right through
To justify the things I do

Each thought coils upon the last
Slithering from sinful past
It shames me, knowing God can see
How wicked my own thoughts can be

The fangs and poison all revealed
The scales that keep my vision sealed
To Jesus I must turn my eyes
To stop these thoughts that paralyze

Constricted lungs can breathe again
As I confess my hidden sin
My fitful mind, again made sound
By He who keeps the serpent bound

Hand Washing

You cannot wash your hands of Jesus
He won't be rinsed off of your skin
To refuse Him simply means
That you will die within your sin

Pontius Pilate, in the Bible
Tried to wash his conscience clean
In reality, he couldn't
God knows all that goes unseen

You may deny Him, or forget Him
Insist you don't want Him around
That doesn't change the fact that Jesus
Wore for you a thorny crown

As He asked God to forgive you
The shame of sin upon His face
Crimson streams of blood escaped Him
As His hands were nailed in place

His precious blood was flowing freely
As it flows for you today
If you accept it for atonement
All your sins will wash away

But don't wash your hands of Jesus
That none perish is His goal
If you decide to live without Him
You are forfeiting your soul

Quickening

Fitful sleep, my nightmares keep
Waking me inside
I make the choice to quench Your voice
Misgivings I must hide

Yet You call, so still and small
A whisper shouting through
I turn my head as words You've said
Within my soul ring true

On I run, the damage done
For miles I don't look back
But You keep pace and offer grace
Each time I get off track

I ignore Your open door
And jump out of my skin
Chilled to the bone, my comfort zone
Is quickly wearing thin

My conscience fails, You speak of nails
And blood shed on the cross
Unmasking me that I may see
My Savior suffer loss

You pour in and find my sin
Light shines where all was dim
Oh Spirit please, bend my stiff knees
As I return to Him

Restless nights, internal fights
I will embrace them all
I shed a tear—thank God I hear
The Holy Spirit call

On Bended Knee

Why do I pull away from You
Instead of drawing near?
I stop my ears from letting in
That still, small voice I hear

Down deep, I want to talk with You
and bow on bended knee
But the world and its surroundings
Have a strange appeal to me

Dear Lord, help me to break away
From temptation and its hold
I used to praise You constantly
But now my tongue's grown cold

It hurts me so to open up
I feel I should confess
But then I'd have to talk about
My sins and all the rest

I get so tired of running
Because I know You'll win the race
For even in my sins
You pardoned me with saving grace

Here I stand in deep repentance
Chains are falling at my feet
And the praises on my tongue
Have never tasted quite so sweet

Lord, I ask for Your forgiveness
For my foolishness and pride
For losing faith in God the Father
For my hardened heart inside

Oh my Jesus, show great mercy
On this selfish soul of mine
Let me serve You once again Lord
Cause my heart to beat with Thine

Nowhere to Run

Can I run away from the earth or the sky?
Hide my face from each second of time passing by?

Shall I empty my lungs and refuse to breathe air?
Deny gentle winds as they dance through my hair?

Ignore both my hunger and thirst from inside?
Find refuge beyond my own body to hide?

Fail to acknowledge the moon, stars, or sun?
Forfeit the daybreak before it's begun?

Not notice the people around me each day?
Close my eyes upon loved ones and wish them away?

How can I run from the twilight now falling?
Or hide from Your still and small voice, always calling?

To lose everything that this human life brings
Is to run from a God who exists in all things.

Misplaced Peace

There is a peaceful place within
Filled with a quiet calm
Soothing to the spirit
As a softly singing Psalm

I rarely visit anymore
I fear I've lost the way
No time for restoration
In my busy day-to-day

I'm holding blindly to this life
Soul seared beyond degree
Hooked by choice into the earth
(Or are its hooks in me?)

A tired and starving prisoner
My insides boil and churn
My cruel, villainess captor is
The world in which I turn

I knew a quiet peace within
A place where healing flows
Can I find my way again?
My Father only knows

Misguidance

I quench the Holy Spirit
Forgetting who I am
With nothing to adhere it
My life's a proven sham

I choose not to remember
The love that made me whole
Feeling an empty recess
Enveloping my soul

Hungry for Your righteousness
Afraid to know Your will
I know how much You care for me
But yet I falter, still

When I ignore Your guiding hand
A crooked path I see
What happens to the ones that for
Their guidance, look to me?

Master Locksmith

I saw him there staring through my window sheers
Trying to rouse and provoke my worst fears

I dared to stare back—I was safe and secure
The front door was shut and locked tight, I was sure

What was he doing out there on my step?
Hoping to find where my treasures were kept?

With puzzled bemusement I watched as he paced
His eyes quickly darkened—my heart quickly raced

He stretched forth his fingers, but rang not the bell
His hand held an object that my eyes knew well

He smirked and he winked as he leered in at me
Mouthing the words, "Thanks for leaving your key"

I ransacked each pocket as ice filled each vein
He held up my house key and jingled the chain

His foothold was strong as he made his way in
"The key to your soul takes the shape of your sin"

Lights Out

I smile within Your light by day
Darkness fills my heart by night

My spirit whispers to my soul
That something's just not right

In illuminated mornings
Each day is bright and clear

But waking in the midnight hour
Your still, small voice I hear

How I need Your light, Lord
To keep me free from sin

But spotlight me from Heaven, please
My lamp's unplugged within

It needed energy to glow
So I pulled out the cord

The price to pay attention
More than I could afford

My mind would rather wander
To where it shouldn't be

So lend Your nightlight to me, Lord
There's no light left in me

Good Morning, Goodbye

With each morning's sunrise God's mercies are new
His grace is sufficient to carry me through
The Lord calls me to Him, to meet heart to heart
To renew my mind with His daily fresh start

Why must I sleep through Your sweet break of day
Ignoring Your voice as my thoughts go astray
How many moments have I let tick past
While chasing the dreams that I knew would not last

Missing the whispers breathed into my soul
The refreshing of spirit that makes my life whole
I've missed words of wisdom to share with a friend
My prayer life collapses on knees that won't bend

I long for the warmth of Your Fatherly touch
A firm rock to stand on in place of my crutch
In the cool of the morning my Savior draws nigh
Will I rise to greet Him, or bid Him goodbye?

Giving In

I am in His house
Though not on bended knee
Nothing seems to rouse
The soul that sleeps in me

Holy ground I feel
It burns beneath my feet
I know that He is real
Yet, backward I retreat

Pastor does his best
To wake me up inside
But life's lull-a-bye
Sings softly to my pride

It should be enough
To feel His presence here
Diamond in the rough
When will my shine appear?

To accept His grace
Would mean my giving in
Can I stand and face
The One who forgives sin?

I am in His house
Lord, help me bend my knee
I pray, don't let me douse
The fire that sets me free

Father Called

My Father calls me
I am too busy to come…
Please call back

My Father calls me
I am too tired to wake…
Try later

My Father calls me
I fear what He has to say…
I'm not home

My Father calls me
The noise in my head is loud…
I can't hear

My Father calls me
I do not answer His call…
His voice stills

Faithing Famine

I've made a new discovery; you're sure to be amazed
An appetite suppressant worthy to be praised

Sure it makes you shaky, you might forget your name
But your hunger will subside (extinguishing your flame)

Its side effects are many; its benefits are few
It's habit forming—but it works—in just a dose or two

There is no pill to swallow, just pour it in your eyes
Fill them up with worldly cares, and soon they'll magnetize

Your hunger will diminish; in fact, you'll grow quite thin
Inside your spirit withers while your soul grows fat with sin

Suppress your thirst for righteousness, your hunger for the Lord
The cost of slimming down your faith? More than you can afford

Daze Away

I am undeserving of this day
The sun should shine upon a sweeter soul
Within me where the human eye is blind
A bitter attitude has taken toll

My insides are a lonely shade of blue
I turn the rumpled pages of my mind
I wonder what the Lord has found in me
Dislike for who I am is all I find

I look beyond my window at the birds
They mock me with the beauty they possess
Enjoying life, as God has called them to
Wiser are the birds than me, I guess

Counting reasons why I don't deserve
The glory of the day that waits outside
My eyes grow heavy and I fall asleep
But in my dream, my eyes are open wide

I dream of sunny skies and birds of song
They sing to me as I run through the grass
A freedom fills me as I just accept
The blessings that through God have come to pass

I wake up and I smile to greet the sun
But now the light is gone and all is dark
I've slept right through another God-sized day
On which I could have left the Savior's mark

Circus Life

I put on my mask
And hide shakily behind
The smile of a clown

Struggling for balance
I teeter helplessly on
This tightrope of pride

Do not closely look
To conceal my features
I'd risk a great fall

More than meets the eye
See the marionette dance
In this tent of flesh

Alone With Me

Alone with ears too wise to hear
And eyes to blind to see
Dear Lord Jesus, please don't leave
Myself alone with me

In darkness vengeance steals my thoughts
And rolls within my head
I taste the words I long to say
Words better left unsaid

My twisting, turning, twiddling thumbs
Will not be bored for long
Bad habits jump into my hands
Where soon they will grow strong

My feet will run to Trouble's door
And beg to come inside
Where they will roam forbidden halls
Built up by foolish pride

Lord, please stay beside me now
God hear my humble plea
I'm formed of dust, and just can't trust
Myself alone with me

Crawl

Would a father tell a toddler, when first shaky steps begin,

"Little child, now that you're walking, you can never crawl again!
You must never trip nor stumble, never fall down on the floor
For if you crawl instead of walking—you will be my child no more."

When unstable ground consumes us, at times we all collapse and fall
God in Heaven is our Father, extending mercy to us all
Jesus Christ does not abandon, He reaches out His caring hand
And if we hold our grasp around it, we will rise once more and stand

Grasping Freedom

When I walk with my Father
He always leads the way
Hand in hand my steps are sure
If by His side I stay

We walk and talk a little while
But soon I turn my eyes
Distractions fill my foolish mind
I'm chasing butterflies

With one twist of my sweaty hand
I break grip and run free
I cross the street all by myself
With no one helping me!

But now the butterflies are gone
And I'm all on my own
I look over my shoulder
I guess Father walked alone

I wanted to taste freedom
Waving both hands in the wind
Now I'm lost, so far from home
By breaking free, I've sinned

The freedom in my Father's will
Is perfect by design
Found only when the hand of God
Is firmly grasped in mine

Self

Self-centered Christian
Eyes focused in
So self-absorbed
Hiding in my own skin

Self-conscious, I wonder
What they think of me
How filled up with self
Can one selfish soul be?

Self-reliant, self-compliant
Self-sufficient—come what may
Self-help will not help me
Keep myself at bay

Only Jesus can pull out
My self-righteous thorn
Selflessly reminding me
That I'm reborn

Peace of You

I remember back in time when I was free
Finding You was just the key for me
My doors and windows opened—standing wide
I felt You rearranging me inside

Your vision filled my eyes both night and day
I had such urgency to read and pray
Tears fell when I encountered loved ones, lost
I spoke to friends of Your death on the cross

I walked on air, my feet not on the ground
Back when I called Your name and peace was found
Today Your footsteps echo not so near
And when I'm lost, the way seems not so clear

I stand beside the path, narrow and straight
Have I misplaced my key to Entrance Gate?
It must have fallen from my human hand
As my eyes wandered from my Master's plan

Fenced in, I retrace steps to find the place
Where I let go and dropped out of the race
But the change of pace was subtle, and was slow
And my head began to tell me where to go

Soon vanity and pride held high esteem
To flood my soul and pollute the Living Stream
Afraid, I sit surrounded by my sin
I call Your name and feel Your peace again

Amnesia

I remember when You called me
And taught my heart to pray
The sun burst through the mounting clouds
Just the other day

Yesterday I closed my eyes
I longed to hear Your Word
Today my mind cannot recall
Most of what I've heard

I witnessed Your hand moving
In strength my faith did grow
I held my breath in humbled awe
Not so long ago

At times my soul consumed You
I welcomed You with tears
It was a day or two ago
Maybe it's been years

Busy days now fill my life
My peace is all but gone
Will You recognize me Lord
Has it been too long?

I listen for Your still, small voice
That used to clearly speak
Reminding me that You are strong
Whenever I am weak

Familiar tears spill from my eyes
I feel my prayer break through
"My child," You whisper to my soul
"I've not forgotten you."

The Perfect Gift

I received a gift this morning, it was wrapped up with a bow
What would I find inside? I was curious to know

The bow was bright and lovely, I thought to put it in my hair
But it tore as I untied it, then wasn't fit to wear

I gazed upon the paper wrapped around my gift-untold
I'd take the pretty wrapping off, a fan to crease and fold

But the paper ripped to pieces, there would be no homemade fan
Only scraps of tattered paper, lying limply in my hand

The box is all that's left now sitting naked on the floor
Looking plain and lifeless, not enticing like before

But as I opened up the box, so carefully and light
I found the box was empty and I screamed, "This isn't right!"

As I cried amid the ruins sobs were muffling my words
But above my wail and moaning, a still, small voice was heard

"I'm glad you liked My bow of blue, I knew it matched your eyes
I hoped you'd find appealing the special way I had it tied

Your paper was a canvas, painted by My hand
I longed for you to cherish it and smile, as I had planned

The box was yours to treasure, a world of beauty to behold
The space that dwelt within the walls—not to have, but just to hold

For the inside was My vessel; I was to live there, deep within
You eagerly destroyed My gift before you let Me in."

Good Morning, Lord

Good morning, Lord
Your presence urges me to wake
I close my eyes again
Your voice whispers through my soul
Gently breezing through my spirit
Like wind through trees
My thoughts tremble and sway
Helplessly clinging
Like leaves
My heartbeat quickens
I know You're there
I pretend You're not
Afraid for You to read my mind
Terrified for You to know my heart
You already do
I look forward to a day
When thought and spirit are not at war
And love comes naturally
When holiness fortifies
And courses through veins
Like blood
Faith comes in waves
Crashing over me
Drenching my soul
You will return
Walking upon those waves
As You walked on water
That will be a good morning,
Lord

Countdown

Anticipation builds up
As the New Year's Apple falls
The countdown marks an end
Amid the whistles, shouts and calls

Spectators look relieved
To see the year come to a close
In hopes the midnight hour
Will blot out pain, regret, and woes

Some cry lost in emotion
Others seal it with a kiss
Some toast a new day dawning
Others mourn loved ones they miss

Many rush to pencil down
The things they hope to change
But few will hold resolve
When cold winds blow and rearrange

And as we join the countdown
That the world so magnified
Let us remain God's children
For whom our precious Savior died

And remember in this life
No earthly moment can erase
One single sin or deed
This is performed only by grace

A grace God has appointed
Never changing, always true
A pardon freely given
As a sinner's prayer breaks through

Only hearts filled with repentance
Will experience and know
How it feels to face God's countdown
With a heart as white as snow

By Invitation Only

Be kind to them for Me
I heard Father say
Be patient and loving
While leading the way

Be kind to them for Me
For them I have bled
But their hearts have been hardened
So be kind, in My stead

Be kind to them for Me
I won't force Myself in
So please tell them for Me
Of forgiveness from sin

Be kind to them for Me
The unlovable, too
For when you were yet sinners
I gave My life for you

Be kind to them for Me
And never resent
Your merciful ways
May cause souls to repent

Be kind to them for Me
Keep their hope alive
By faith's invitation
I soon will arrive

Letter to Mother

Mother, let me walk alone
Armed with truth and faith you've shown
Through the night I must find my own way

I know you worry and you cry
In darkness sometimes so do I
My frightened tears must not see light of day

I recall our bedtime prayers
We'd pray for people everywhere
And then you'd pray the lost to soon be found

The monsters underneath my bed
Would flee as from God's Word you read
But monsters here just seem to stick around

The hope you gave me still lives on
One day those monsters will be gone
So forward I will march toward that time

This call to serve that pulls me here
Is stronger than my deepest fear
And larger than each mountain I must climb

People sometimes shed a tear
They pat my back and pull me near
With gratitude and pride their voices hoarse

Yet I would die for those as well
Who greet me with an angered yell
Their opposition will not change my course

I have chosen now to lead
Knowing this day I may bleed
With the stench of war upon my skin

Mother, don't cry in your bed
Kneel and pray for me instead
For I am called a soldier among men

Find Your Wings

Soon you will be on your own
The years have gone so fast
Although, to you it may have seemed
That slowly time has passed

Tears of joy and sorrow fall
To mingle on my face
It seems I had but moments to
Enjoy a child's embrace

Now childhood things are packed away
Time's hands I can't detain
But as adulthood draws you near
God's child you will remain

God's seed is sown within your heart
Down deep, where true faith clings
I know your roots are strong enough
To help you find your wings

I pray your memories are clear
And serve you, as they should
Find growth within the painful ones
Find comfort in the good

In faith, I hope your future dreams
Reflect the prayers I've prayed
And that you seek the face of God
In each decision made

May passion beat within your heart
The way you pulse through mine
And may your branches spread the sky
But never leave the Vine

Behind the Scenes

I ran and jumped and skipped and danced
In the freshly mown back lawn
Never noticing who cut the grass
I loved to play upon

But now I know who trims the grass
And keeps it short for play
Wiping sweat from off my brow
I put lawn tools away

Sitting in the middle
Of my grandma's bed, so soft
It never looked as tidy
When my dolls and I crawled off

But now I smooth the wrinkles
From a bed once neatly made
And fluff the floral pillows
Where my daughter's dollies played

Now I spray the stain remover
On the knees of little jeans
No longer playing in the spotlight
Working hard behind the scenes

I pick play dough from the carpet
I swipe fingerprints away
I wash dishes in the kitchen
After cooking meals each day

And I smile inside, just knowing
They enjoy the things I do
And if I should go unnoticed
Perhaps I'll learn a thing or two

About my Father up in Heaven
World Creator, King of Kings
Providing needs I take for granted
Working hard behind the scenes

Attitude of the Heart

The lawn needs mowing—the yard is a mess
The laundry is dirty—I need a new dress

The dishes need washing—there's dinner to make
I'm worn and I'm tired—no time for a break

The children are fighting—their room's a disgrace
I'll never catch up at this snail crawling pace

Maybe I'll stop—let it all fall apart
"What is," asks the Lord, "the attitude of your heart?"

"Is your attitude giving, is your attitude fair?
Is your attitude causing your heart not to care?

Is your attitude angry, is it spiteful and mean?
Has it made you lose faith in God's treasures, unseen?

Has it tainted your spirit, made your countenance fall?
Will your attitude hold any blessings at all?

A house that's divided will never stand strong
You will never find peace if your attitude's wrong."

I stopped my complaining—looked slowly around
I could hardly believe all the blessings I found!

Green grass surrounding our small, modest home
Each room containing memories of its own

I began to remember the times that we'd had
Somehow my chores did not seem so bad

Together we'd dirtied much laundry and dishes
As we laughed, and we cried, and we made birthday wishes

The small things that mean so much in my life
God has given me purpose—as mother and wife

I have found deep inside me a new place to start
A God-given peace—attitude of the heart

Hat Hanger

Pick a nail to hang your hat on
Then firmly hang it there

Be it shiny, be it rusty
Be unique, do not compare

Let the others hang their own hats
Show them your support and care

But forget not where your nail is
From the wall so many stare

If you lose the space you've chosen
You'll hold your hat in deep despair

Hang your hat upon your own nail
Wisely choose the hat you wear

Individuality

Sing your soul
Song placed in your heart
Song of no other

Shed your tears
Uniquely your own
Cry for your brother

Walk your path
The crooks and the bends
Familiar to you

Know yourself
Trust in your spirit
To test what is true

To your God
Each song that you sing
Sounds like no other

Sing your soul
Songs written for you
Not for another

Lot Appreciation

We are issued a foundation
At the moment of our birth
Some are not as firm as others
All need repair upon this earth

We're allotted blocks to build with
Certain there are just too few
Born with fingerprints, not blueprints
Building life is hard to do

But our blocks are custom tailored
Each one formed so carefully
By our Father, in His wisdom
Who shapes a future we can't see

We can curse our pile of rubble
And sit down upon the stones
Or build up a little shelter
For a neighbor's weary bones

With contentment, or resentment
How will you choose to view your lot?
Spotting stable dirt seems harder
Once the Savior's gaze is caught

If your blocks form not a castle
Rest assured as daylight dims
Heaven holds for you a mansion
Crafted from God's finest gems

Gifted

Use the gift God's given you
However big or small
For we know not the day nor hour
When Jesus comes to call

Don't spend a precious moment
Fretting over what you've not
The talents that you do possess
Deserve your time and thought

Sing a little, dance a little
Play a little, if you can
Or speak the blessed words of hope
Unto your fellow man

Share that smile God's given you
With someone who has none
Give of yourself to please our God
Who gave His only son

Rootbound

Shaking out and dusting off the soil
Covering and hiding from the rain
Shrinking from the sunshine, ever loyal
Until the seeds of nothingness remain

Our roots grow intertwined within the earth
We embrace for fear that we will drown
Not holding onto love for all it's worth
But faithfully we hold each other down

Plucking petals as we wilt away
Sharpening our thorns before we go
We can never weed out yesterday
Our empty promises will never grow

Holding hands within the cleansing soil
Opening our hearts up to the rain
Welcoming the sun to cheer our toil
Allowing God to plant us once again

Now Is The Time

Now is the time while our ground is still level
To reach eagerly into ourselves
To shake off the dust that settled upon us
As we sat like stone statues on shelves

Now is the time to roll out those scriptures
Unique and familiar to you
Cover with them like a favorite blanket
Share old warmth with somebody new

Now is the time that we need to remember
To let others walk by God's call
For the Lord knows his steps, let us not intercept
Lest we cause our own brother to fall

Now is the time while we're humble and open
To bypass the usual pew
To rebuild our faith as we rebuild our walls
To see things from a fresh point of view

Now is the time as we work side by side
To be more than a Sunday handshake
We will become better friends by the time this all ends
Building bonds that no church fire can break

Connection

Brothers and sisters, we function as one
Adhered to each other through God's only son

Believers, together, wherever we roam
The faith shared between us will soon take us home

Forgiveness to cover the battles we've fought
No hard feelings linger in deed or in thought

A love dwells inside like a flame burning bright
A brother brings honor; a sister, delight

Many prayers offered up have included your name
And tears of joy fell at your Salvation claim

A warmth comes from knowing you're never alone
Someone stands beside you of same flesh and bone

Eyes on You

I asked the Lord for peace of mind
He told me what to do
Take my eyes off of myself
And place them upon you

So many prideful, selfish thoughts
Build up within my head
I will tear down those wicked walls
And build you up instead

My eyes are always searching
For someone to mistrust
I shall borrow Jesus' eyes
To see you as He must

I'll not dismiss your angry words
By turning you away
I instead will listen close
For what you're trying to say

I do not need to take offense
When we do not agree
Contrary to my nature
I will choose diplomacy

I will strengthen in His spirit
Not by power, nor by might
For I am among those chosen
To distribute salt and light

Examination

"The poor soul," I remark, sadly shaking my head
"If I were like him, I would wish myself dead."
I observe his life, the bad choices he's made
How his selfish demands caused his conscience to fade
It's much too late now, I can see no more hope
As I look at his life through my keen microscope

Fittingly, I've forgotten my own wicked ways
The pain I brought others, regrettable days
It lifts my remorse to seek out your flaws
Holding you to the light, I examine the cause
Judging you as the Pharisee judged in the temple
To keep track of your sin is surprisingly simple

But take heed this warning—at all cost refrain
From bringing up *my* past, if remnants remain
There is vast difference between you and I
Comparability absent, don't even try
In fact, keep your distance—don't come near at all
I'll be at the church, so don't bother to call

For goodness sake, don't hold me up to that light!
I've examined myself, finding I am just right
Besides, if the light gets too close to my skin
You'll surely see ugliness lurking within
My veil will then vanish like smoke on a breeze
Only God knows I praise Him from self-righteous knees

Returning Judgment

Excuse me sir, I must return
An article or two
I'll simply never use them
Although Satan wants me to

I have this robe and gavel
Much used in days gone by
When I concerned myself with specks
Within my brother's eye

Now his eyes shine brightly
Washed clean before the throne
While I sit tweezing splinters
From the board within my own

I've criticized and whispered
Time now to face God's test
Judged by the very measures
That I used to judge the rest

God knows I'll never measure up
My heart will come up short
If only I had loved in truth
Not as a last resort

So put these items on your shelf
Beside your sticks and stones
I'll leave the judging to the God
Who forms dust into bones

It Takes One to Know One

It seems this shallow heart of mine
Is lifted from despair
As I hold others to the light
And to myself compare

They are weak and I am strong
Superior, am I
No way for them to measure up
How dare they even try

I turn my nose up at their sin
I loudly judge their ways
May God have mercy on my soul
When justly, He repays

Quitting My Day Job

I'm quitting my day job
God knows it's not right
To be a judge in the daytime
And a Christian at night

I've heard sordid stories
Too strange to believe
I've kept them in mind
So I could retrieve

Of course as a judge
I would always comply
By throwing two cents in
With no reason why

But God took my gavel
And gave me a mirror
Where I saw a sinner
Revoltingly clear

I'm quitting my day job
No notice to give
For I will be judged
By the life that I live

Vision

I own a pair of glasses
My God crafted them by hand
They correct my blurry vision
Though the world can't understand

I put on my special glasses
To focus on what God would see
In the faces of the people
He has put in touch with me

I can see beyond their anger
And hurtful words that so offend
Beneath the calluses are tender
Broken hearts afraid to mend

Sometimes I forget my glasses
And I judge with turned up nose
Later I repent in sorrow
As denial's rooster crows

I'm so thankful, God in Heaven
Has such special vision too
For without it I would never
Measure up or follow through

God's great vision is so holy
He sees this child through eyes of grace
Upon His palms, my loving Father
Placed the image of my face

There are times I fail to witness
Afraid to practice what I preach
Lord, remind me every day
To keep my glasses within reach

Sponge

Absorb the pain of others
Blot and dry their tears
Wipe their doubts then wring them out
Mop away their fears

Keep surroundings spic and span
Including thoughts and deeds
Scrub beneath the surface where
Resentment often breeds

Dependable, reusable
"Serve Me," the Good Lord said
Too bad for all, I missed the call
I'm self-absorbed instead

Speak No Evil

Our tongues praise our Lord and Father
Then they curse our fellow men
Chapter three, verse nine, of James
Reveals the danger of this sin

Speaking badly about others
Is speaking ill of God as well
For we're all formed in His image
He designed each last detail

Can fresh water and saltwater
Ever flow from the same spring?
How can we put down another
While lifting up our Holy King?

Let's show mercy to each other
With our words and with our deeds
Let's not speak behind the back
But follow where the spirit leads

When we walk with Christ the Savior
For evil words there are no place
Appointed time is soon arriving
When we'll meet Him face to face

Listen

There is a time to listen
And a time to lend an ear
Those who listen more
Are blessed by what they hear

Listen without judging
It's amazing what you'll learn
You'll hear the Holy Spirit
As He helps your soul discern

Listen very closely
For clues behind each word
Listen for the heartfelt cry
Perhaps no one has heard

Listen without thinking
Of the next word you will say
You were humbly called of God
To love others today

So listen with your inner heart
To needful souls around
It may enable them to hear
The Lord's last trumpet sound

Life Changers

I look for Life Changers
Behind every tree
Those who encourage
Frown-finders like me

Planted by streams
With their roots running deep
Life Changers watch closely
While all others sleep

They love introducing
A new point of view
Christ-filled and dynamic
With words that hold true

Life Changers are busy
And never waste time
On big earthly mountains
Too unsound to climb

Not fearful of danger
On Faith's feet they tread
Not clinging to custom
But changing, instead

Ignite

Holy Fire, burn—explode in my bones!
Singe evils within me Your blood did atone

Burn up my defenses, and wicked pride too
Consume with Your fire all that displeases you

Let Your smoke billows protect me from shame
Set my tongue upon fire as I shout out Your name

My conceit turn to ashes, my will into soot
Burn the seeds of temptation before they take root

Set Your holy flames on me, as burning I run
To spread forth Your fire and engulf everyone

Place within me no embers, only flames burning bright
Pour fire into me, Lord, my spirit ignite

Fly

Fly, my precious children
Unfold your cherished wings
Foolish pride held mine inside
With the fear of worldly things

But children, you are different
With wide, embracing eyes
Challenges met without regret
Prepare your wings to fly

If I could only show you
How to soar among the stars
Why did I wait—is it too late
To leave my prison bars?

I'll do my best to teach you
To remain honest and true
Fly where you might, but do what's right
Take time to think things through

Keep a heart that's ever tender
Keep an open, gentle ear
My little birds, please heed my words
Never fly away from fear

Greet fear while facing forward
Never expose your back
Fear knows your cares and lingers there
Your weakness to attack

Please take these pearls of wisdom
From Mother's broken wings
Reach far, fly high, make yours the sky
But nest beside the King

Hungry Hearts

Full hearts are always hungry
They're never satisfied
They search the world for empty souls
And fill them up inside

Full hearts are always pumping
They liven up your day
Forever cheering others on
With special words they say

Full hearts take not for granted
The warmth of outstretched hands
They find the strength to pull you up
And never make demands

Full hearts give God the glory
For hunger-pangs within
An appetite for Jesus Christ
Will save the soul from sin

Encouragement

Sweeping forth in conversation
Tumbling out of God's Word
Rising from literature's printed page
Exhaling from a whispered prayer
Drifting up through the clutter of my television set
Singing directly into my trembling soul

Each word a portrait framed by hope

Speak
The word you release may fill the blank space upon my wall
Speak

My soul awaits your masterpiece

De-Face

Do not witness to my eyes
My tears, rehearsed, can fool the wise

Don't be swindled by my grin
Who says your words are sinking in?

Attentive ears perk up with ease
In one…out of other…if you please

Expressions change as seconds bound
My face is not your lost and found

The physical will ebb and flow
Seeds placed with the spirit grow

So minister to what's inside
Pray for the Holy Spirit guide

Converse with me on level ground
Where His anointed words resound

Don't try to read what's on my face
Speak to my soul, His saving grace

Windows

I long to open windows, to breathe the fresh clean air
So many windows I've ignored, forgetting they are there

Clutter laden windowsills block out the panes of time
Windows I need desperately to pray, and read, and rhyme

Cobwebs lace the window frames of opportunity
The dust upon the glass, so thick, my dreams I cannot see

A few I have left open but the air is never sweet
Rain pours in the gaping holes of judgment and deceit

The windows made for witnessing have all been painted shut
I can't break through to others for the fear of getting cut

May New Year's Day

May the smile of a child cause your dry eyes to gleam
May the joy of your spirit be as a sweet dream

May bygones be bygones without one regret
May we model our Savior—forgive and forget

May all slamming doors jar the windows right up
May the blessings spill over when God fills your cup

May heartstrings be many and heartaches be few
May time be a friend, not a bandit to you

May Christmas embrace you and dance you away
May all troubles vanish, at least for the day

May you feel God's presence and know that He's near
May Christ fill your heart as you greet the New Year

Someone's Watching

If I'd known you were watching
I would have taken care
To start each morning seeking God
Instead of what to wear

If I'd known you were watching
I would have found a way
To minister God's Word to you
Within my busy day

If I'd known you were watching
My gossip would have ceased
Hearsay's careless whisperings
I would have not released

If I'd know you were watching
With conviction, I'd have cried
As I explained that for your sins
Our Lord was crucified

If I'd known you were watching
Christ's seed I would have sown
You would have found eternal life
If I had only known

Give a Little

Make room for the third wheel
Who seems to slow your pace
If you attach an extra wheel
You might just win the race

When others want to share the warmth
That you possess within
Thank God His light is shining bright
Right through your selfish skin

If someone standing near you
Loves basking in your glow
Be thankful, not resentful
Share the stage, don't steal the show

Behold the bit-part players
Mere flowers on your wall
You'll someday find without them
You are nothing, after all

Indifference

I stand strongly, safe and sound
Planted firmly on the ground

My nails dig so deeply in
Holding back my hands from sin

Victory I do not know
I want to fly, but won't let go

I can't reach out—I'll lose my place
No mercy for the human race

They may judge me, they may mock
Instead, I'll stay under my rock

I'll let others lead the way
My comfort zone is where I'll stay

I don't care if others see
The light God placed inside of me

I'll store it up and never tell
Then I'll shine brightly in my shell

My mind is closed; my lips are sealed
Lifesaving secret not revealed

Who cares if someone's lost at sea?
They'll never hitch a ride from me!

My fishing boat, safely at dock
I'm sound asleep beneath my rock

Salt-Seasoned Grace

The world in which I live today
Unfit, unclean, impure
Offenses hurling left and right
Meant just for me, I'm sure

Corruption festers in my ears
And dirt assaults my eyes
Breathing odors of decay
I feel my anger rise

I leap upon my soapbox
To make sure I am seen
But just an empty soapbox
Can't wash anybody clean

I boil and spew with anger
God's face I do not seek
My tongue is strong in judgment
In spirit, I am weak

Remind me yet again, Lord
With shame upon my face
Souls are not won by fits of rage
But by salt-seasoned grace

Stones

Stones, so easy to pick up
Even easier to throw
Some stones are tossed behind the back
By loved ones that you know

Other stones are saved and gathered
"Ammunition" so to speak
Used by vengeful souls
Too proud to turn the other cheek

At times a stone must be dug up
Before it can be thrown
A shameful past reminder
Tossed about by Satan's own

Gossip is a shiny stone
Too precious not to share
Watch the wide eyes gleaming
As it takes flight in thin air

Stones are many sizes
Pebbles, boulders, and between
Some judge and throw accordingly
At every person seen

Is it a big sin, or a small sin?
I'll surely find a stone that fits
I'm the self-appointed judge
Who casts the stones, and never quits

Let he who remains sinless
Throw the stone he's holding first
All of humankind is sin-filled
Freed by Jesus from our curse

So before you pick your stone up
Taking aim at those around
Satan wishes first to thank you
With your help, he's gaining ground

Pass or Fail

How can you ensure
You're nice to be around
A friendship to be found
Your kindness does abound?

If you do not endure
The unlovable as well
The ones that scream and yell
The scoffers who rebel?

Does Satan use his lure
Whispering his lie
Causing you to cry
To roll your eyes and sigh?

Are your thoughts impure
You talk behind the back
Cut other men no slack
Plan vengeful attack?

Remember where you were
When Jesus took you in
And washed away your sin
He changed your focus then

Judge others and be sure
He will judge you the same
A mark beside your name
You will look down in shame

A humble heart's the cure
For smugness and conceit
Pride comes before defeat
Repent, and sins retreat

Believers now mature
Build up your fellow man
Your selfish notions ban
Love is the Master's plan

Let God's convictions stir

Follow The Leader

Don't follow my leading
It leads to nowhere
I've nothing without God
Not even a care

I've no friends without Him
No family tree
My loved ones are God's own
He shares them with me

Don't walk in my footsteps
Or wish for my place
My every possession
Reflects my Lord's face

He made me an offer
I couldn't refuse
To follow the Leader
And walk in His shoes

Foolishness

The message of the cross
Is foolishness to these
Who quickly now are perishing
The souls who don't believe

But to the true believer
It is the power of God
To those of us saved by the blood
By foolishness we're called

The foolishness of God
Confounds the wisest mind
True power and true wisdom
Are by our faith defined

Be unapologetic
When ridiculed by man
Use foolish understanding
To wisely take a stand

A Friend In Deed

I LONG TO TEAR THE ROOF OFF

climb the walls
rise above
for the lost souls that I love

TO HEAR THE RIPPING OF THE TILES

in my ears
all around
as light shines through on the ground

TO LOOK DOWN AND SEE THE OTHERS

in the house
faces cold
wondering who could be so bold

AND SEE JESUS LOOKING UP

mercy great
now revealed
soul soon saved and body healed

TO LOWER DOWN A FRIEND IN NEED

Jesus speaks
forgiving sin
the paralyzed can walk again

Shedding Shadows

Thank You, God, for this bright morning
I pray You'll help me live it right
Not to spend it casting shadows
But to spend it shedding light

Let me speak no passing judgments
Casting shadows filled with doubt
Let my voice be soft and even
With no mumbling or shout

Let me cause someone to giggle
Joy escaping from their lips
To forget their toil and trouble
Pain that holds them in its grip

Father, let me be a blessing
Let Your light shine out to all
Let my heart reflect Your mercy
Humble me each time I fall

Do not allow me to cast shadows
Or to cause my brother strife
Let shedding light become my mission
As I model Jesus' life

Soul Mate

Some say you reach a man's heart with possessions
I believe his heart is reached a different way
I believe a heart is touched through understanding
Through experience we're given day by day

I believe inside we're looking to each other
To try and find a similarity
To find a friend who knows us like no other
Someone who understands the self we long to be

Experiences vary with each person
Who claims to know the source of every pain?
Exists a man who lives your every moment
He was killed, and buried
Then He rose again!

The man I know sticks closer than a brother
The man I know has shared your every breath
He's felt the depth of every known emotion
He is the only living man to endure death

So if you hope to find a loving soulmate
A heart of understanding beating true
Remember that you have a friend in Jesus
He knows the hidden man alive in you

Mind Reader

God says, "Fear not their faces," still I maintain my fear
I dread the way they look at me when it's my voice they hear

I must be a mind reader, it seems I always know
What's taking place in other's thoughts, my apprehension grows

I know just what they're thinking—the words they long to say
I know inside they're judging me, and filing me away

Sometimes I feel so paralyzed within this social fear
Always walking upon eggshells until my path's no longer clear

Adopting attitudes too often, not standing firmly to defend
My identity is fading, where do they end and I begin?

I ask the Lord for guidance and I call upon His grace
He reminds me I cannot read minds, for it is not my place

My place is to see others with eyes merciful and kind
It is not my job to worry about the faults that others find

Concerning myself only with the faults God finds in me
Will break the hold I've given men, and set my spirit free

Self-Control

Throw a temper tantrum, quit my job and walk away
I know that I could do it, but I choose not to today

Cut off that crazy driver, steal a person's parking spot
Free will is mine, but I'll decide to do as Jesus taught

What would people think of her, if they knew what I'd heard?
Today I'll choose to hold my tongue and not repeat a word

I had the right to tell him off—he started yelling first!
Next time I'll choose composure, not to be seen at my worst

Each day is filled with choices, so there's never an excuse
God blessed our lives with self-control—a gift we all should use

Offense

How quickly words can build us up; how quickly we fall down
How many times we kick ourselves when no one is around

How often do we judge ourselves with opinions of another?
How much time is wasted while we're "sizing up" each other?

How does a glare or rude remark spoil my entire day?
How can someone's persuasion change the words I mean to say?

Why do we pay such notice to a stranger's prying eye?
Do we have time to take offense while life is passing by?

Isn't the day the Lord has made, a gift to all who live?
If we could operate in love, would our hearts soon forgive—

Transgressions of people we know, and mistakes we make ourselves?
Could we cast out spoiled yesterdays still sitting on our shelves?

To see others with God's vision is the peaceful thing to do
Remember, those offending you are only human too

Grandma, Twice Visited

She is unaware
Her words jump forth, wounding me
Without cause

My tongue burns with wrath
Held in place by God's wisdom
I sit still

I knock once again
Her voice is comfortably soft
I listen

Her words soothe my ears
They are as music to me
My soul smiles

Home Sweet Home

A hug from my son—he's getting so big
He says, "I love you, Mom"
My beautiful daughter kisses my cheeks
While holding my face in her palms

The cute little dog belongs to my son
But seems to think I am his mother
I give my husband a kiss goodnight
We smile and embrace one another

I lie down in the dark, my heart so content
A tear escapes down my face
When I look at my family, I see the reflection
Of my Father's great mercy and grace

The love of another is blessing enough
To last till the end of my days
But God saw it fit to bless me much more
By giving me children to raise

I may never receive one more day on this earth
God knows when my departure will be
But whenever I leave, there'll be peace in my soul
Knowing all in my house so loved me

Love's Rainbow

God made a promise to us all
His rainbow is the sign
God also sealed a special bond
Between your heart and mine

After He sent the mighty flood
That covered all the earth
He brought forth seed for grass and trees
Fresh air, blue skies, new birth

He did the same within my life
When brutal storms blew past
The tender bud of love awoke
With promise made to last

My eyes were opened to the joy
God planted all around
The fragrant blooms drink in the sun
Nature sings its perfect sound

He made in you a caring heart
With extra room for me
He planned for us to fall in love
Where we'll forever be

So when the clouds are moving in
And the skies are bleak and gray
My brow may furrow at the thoughts
That on my mind can weigh

But then I think about our Lord
And His special gift of love
The multicolored splendor
Shining in the sky above

The promise of the rainbow
Is etched upon my heart
He will shelter me within your love
Before the raindrops start

Mother, May I

Mother, may I thank you for sacrificing sleep
For waking up to hold me when in darkness, I did weep

Mother, may I mention how much you mean to me
Without your gentle guiding hands, I don't know where I'd be

Mother, may I help you the way you helped me so
By searching deep within my heart for things I couldn't show

Mother, may I reach you as you reached me inside
You taught me to be humble, my faith never to hide

Mother, may I praise you with honor undefiled
Mother, may God bless you, for rising up His child

A Dad

A dad pours his son's foundation
Into a strong and steady mold
Son receives concrete beginnings
To stand upon as he grows old

A dad tells his pigtailed daughter
She's a princess in his eyes
Daughter treasures Dad's approval
And seeks no glory from the guys

A dad's work is hard and steady
Joy fills the heart of his wife
Provides a good home for his children
Exemplifies strength with his life

No human being can be perfect
A dad lives as though he can
Devoting himself as a father
Upholding virtue as a man

Crossover

There will be no cross in Heaven
Hanging on my mansion wall
When I fellowship with Jesus
I'll have no need for one at all

Rusty nails and splintered wood
Those things that perish won't be found
Like that beloved hymn assures us,
We'll exchange crosses for crowns

I will never be reminded
Of my dreadful sinful past
I will not remember sorrow
Or the darkness that it cast

The unjustified affliction
That my Savior bore for me
Paid the price of my Salvation
'Twas His death that set me free

When we take our place in Heaven
The blessed hope will be fulfilled
We'll never stray the straight and narrow
Tear nor blood will there be spilled

I will hold hands with my Father
Look into His caring face
I will thank Him for His mercy
For His healing and His grace

He'll be surrounded by His children
None will have a cross to bear
The cross was fashioned on the earth
And I believe we'll leave it there

So look for Jesus in the distance
Standing on a cloud divine
When you claim your crown in Heaven
You can leave your cross behind

Glimpse

Just a tiny little peek
I promise not to stare
The smallest glance is all I need
A glimpse of things up there

Is it true the streets are paved
With pure and shining gold?
And people have new bodies that
Will never more grow old?

Do the angels really fly
With wings as white as snow?
And will we somehow recognize
The friends we used to know?

Will Jesus hold me to His chest
And welcome me inside?
Then lead me to my mansion's door
The home where I'll reside?

It seems a fantasy to me
This limitless reward
Absent from this dying earth
Together with my Lord

Sensing Heaven

The sight most precious to behold
A vision I embrace whole-souled
I find in eyes that I love best
When love for me he has professed
(So shall my eyes see in Heaven)

A sound that I most love to hear
The chimes that gently kiss my ear
Are nestled in another's voice
When by my words he does rejoice
(So shall my ears hear in Heaven)

The taste still lingers on my lips
I smile and lick my fingertips
Looking on with plate-sized eyes
As Grandma slices fresh baked pies
(So shall be my taste of Heaven)

Falling leaves warmed by the sun
With open arms my senses run
Through the autumn-scented bliss
To the afternoon of Love's first kiss
(So shall be fragrance of Heaven)

The touch is soft upon my skin
I close my eyes and drink it in
He puts my palm inside his own
Through healing hands his love is shown
(So is the touch of my Savior)

My Favorite Part of Heaven

I know Heaven will be wonderful, a place beyond compare
And every joy we dream about, and more, will greet us there

Sometimes I try to visualize the way my life will be
I picture all my loved ones who are waiting there for me

But if I were to choose the most exciting part of all
I'd choose the part where all my troubles flee when Jesus calls

I so anticipate the time when worries dwell no more
The manmade pressures of this world end at my mansion's door

Long gone will be the scars of emotions, scrapes and cuts
No need to mourn what might have been, no unproductive ruts

No time limits to rush me by, no clock to set or wind
My favorite part of Heaven is my promised peace of mind

The Last Song

In movies on the silver screen
The sweetest song is saved
For "Happily Ever After" scenes
When the hero smiles and waves

The ending seems so bittersweet
You sigh and shed a tear
And as the couple rides away
A love song you can hear

The melody of heartstrings
Is the one that's saved for last
It seems to hold your future
And sweet memories of past

As the music tells the story
Of a loss turned victory
I'm reminded of my future
When Christ will return for me

For you know, Christ is my hero
And for me the war was won
I now anticipate the chorus
Saved for last, by God's own son

Ascension

Someday I will call Heaven home
This earth I'll leave behind
I now can see, by saving grace
Though once my eyes were blind

Streets paved with the purest gold
I hope to one day see
But most of all I long to feel
The change God makes in me

Harbored fears within me
Cease to exist at all
Guilty shackles of regret
Shall break their grasp and fall

My mouth will form no angry words
Despair will be cast out
The joy within my newfound skin
Will leave no room for doubt

Receive me quickly, Heaven
Pearly gates thrown open wide
My vain and selfish worldly cares
Forever cast aside

Hurrying Home

I release my earthly cares
The heaviness that holds me down
I float—I fly
My spirit-wings brushing the sky
Hurrying home
To meet my Maker

As I soar the tethers snap
Falling useless to the ground
I'm loose—I'm free
My strongholds torn asunder
Hurrying home
To meet my Father

I am caught quickly away
Clouds roll back to clear my path
I laugh—I sing
Leaving a world absent of good
Hurrying home
To meet my Savior

Come Inside

As a child, sad tears I cried
When father said to, "Come inside"

All the fun and games would end
Spoiling my world of *Let's Pretend*

Warm summer nights sure made it hard
To leave the world of my backyard

But in the twinkling of an eye
I'll wave my very last goodbye

No time to stick around and play
All make believe will end that day

The bank vault with its bolts and locks
Will fold up like a cardboard box

Lost pieces of a shattered game
Are houses, cars, fortune and fame

A world so fond of hide-and-seek
While counting down, will turn to peek

And this time I'll be smiling wide
When Father says to, "Come inside"

Father's Home

No foundation of stone yet His house stands alone
By the strength of my Father's sheer will
Dwelling place in the air, someday meeting me there
Is a promise He's sure to fulfill

Not one thing of this earth will delay my new birth
When the clouds are rolled back as a scroll
How my heart aches to know that my God loves me so
And He's anchored this pledge to my soul

No mothers weak-kneed beside empty swings
Swaying slowly on days without breeze
Children will smile at strangers without hidden dangers
And play games wherever they please

Elders will find respect with no chance of neglect
Of the darkness there will be no fear
For the light's always on, all black shadows are gone
When the hand of my Father is near

Brushing Fire

I'm still finger painting, my outlines crudely shaking
I turn and face the One who does inspire

It's my desire, to be a portrait of the One who paints with fire

To give my heart, to give my mind
To shed the scales which keep me blind
I must lay all at His feet
Before my portrait is complete

He shall require a soul prepared to paint with Holy Fire

My colors now are fading, my features need re-shading
At times I feel my will could soon retire

I so admire, the strength held by the One who paints with fire

I spill out and He pours in
Eternal flames ignite within
I pray that I may someday touch
The tip of His fire-wielding brush

I'll soon acquire the passion of the One who paints with fire

Lord, take me higher
Paint over me with Your redeeming fire

Whole and entire
Immerse me in the One who paints with fire

ABOUT THE AUTHOR

Anna Marie Kittrell works as a middle school secretary in her beloved Oklahoma hometown where she resides with her high school sweetheart-turned-husband, Tim. She has written for as long as she can remember, and still has many of her tattered creations—stories she used to sell on the playground for a dime, written on notebook paper. Her love of storytelling has grown throughout the years, and she's thrilled her books are now worth more than ten cents.

Find more of Anna's books online at Amazon.

Connect with Anna at Annakittrellauthor.com

Made in the USA
Columbia, SC
20 September 2022

67648728R00122